## Praise for *Be*

MW00416318

*Be Happy No Matter What* *speaks to the truth that, to c* *lives is a function of how we feel about ourselves. Ellen offers techniques to identify and change core self-concepts, to connect with our Inner Wisdom, to be fully present, to choose happiness, to be the author of our lives, and to make it a best seller. It is an easy read packed with pearls of eternal wisdom which, when applied, can't help but improve the quality of our lives."*

**Walter E Jacobson, MD**
Psychiatrist, Speaker & Author of *Forgive To Win!*

*People who have the power to change their thinking have the power to change their lives.* Be Happy No Matter What *is a great blueprint for learning to think differently about anything and everything. It's easily readable and incredibly utilitarian; a must-read for anyone who wants to feel great and get more out of life!*

**Pamela A. Popper**, Ph.D., N.D., The Wellness Forum

*Ellen, thank you for creating such a powerful work! This ground breaking style of writing provides new thoughts to try on and creates an easy and soothingly pain free way to outgrow obsolete thoughts and beliefs that have been limiting your inner freedom and blocking your path to happiness.*

**Allyson Byrd**, Best Selling Author and Transformational Coach

Be Happy No Matter What *carries one of my favorite qualities in a book: it is an easy read - maybe deceptively easy because it offers such deep truths and practical ready-to-use ideas in a sauntering pace. Ellen's examples are interesting and relevant, and invite the reader to find answers to life's challenges within.*

**David Hartman**, LCSW, The Wellness Institute,
Author – *Collecting Lessons*

*I heard Ellen's voice as I read her book,* Be Happy No Matter What, *it is such a beautiful sweet gift to the reader. I love how she takes the reader on an inner journey, speaking to the sub-conscious as well as conscious self, gently inspiring self-compassion as the voyage unfolds. I have to say that I couldn't put it down. I let the words wrap around me like a warm blanket of encouragement and clarity to find my way.*

**Cynthia Webb**, MSSA, LISW-S, Clinical Social Worker, Community Lecturer, Trainer, and Past Executive Director NASW, Ohio Chapter

# Be Happy No Matter What

## 5 Steps to Inner Freedom

# Ellen Seigel

Be Happy No Matter What
5 Steps to Inner Freedom
By Ellen Seigel
Clear Path Publishing
Published by Clear Path Publishing, Columbus, OH

Editor: Lori Zue, www.LoriZueEdits.com
Cover and Interior design: Bella Guzmán, www.HighwireCreative.com
Author Photograph: Lee Seigel

Library of Congress Control Number: 2012941898
ISBN: 978-0-9857623-0-8

ATTENTION CORPORATIONS, UNIVERSITIES, COLLEGES, AND PROFESSIONAL ORGANIZATIONS: Quantity discounts are available on bulk purchases of this book for educational, gift purposes, or as premiums for increasing magazine subscriptions or renewals. Special books or book excerpts can also be created to fit specific needs. For information, please contact Clear Path Publishing, 6161 Busch Blvd., Suite 120, Columbus, OH 43229, 614-842-4374.

# DEDICATION

To my husband, who has witnessed my living and has unconditionally supported my growth since I was sixteen. I am so grateful to you, my love.

To my son, Lee, and daughter-in-law, Kristen. As brilliant, caring, gentle, generous, and competent teachers of philosophy and literature, they have provided for me wonderful, corrective experiences so that I may overcome childhood learning insecurities and thus own my confidence and competence as a student of life...lifting freely to learn, learn, learn. You guys are the best.

To my sister Eileen who I love so much. Thank you for your steady loving presence, and for teaching me the meaning of true caring and patience in intentionally developing relationships. I am grateful for the gift of your love and friendship. Thanks Sis.

# ACKNOWLEDGMENTS

I am grateful to many people who were instrumental in the birthing of this book. Thanks so much to my writing coach and mentor, Jan B. King; my early editor, Christine Soto; my final editor, Lori Zue of Lori Zue Editing Services; my book designer, Bella Guzmán of Highwire Creative; my publishing coordinator and author's assistant, Janica Smith of AdminiSmith; my virtual assistant Patty Kimball of Kimball Business Solutions; and Meredith and Corey Liepelt, owners of Rich Life Marketing.

Thanks also to my friends who are near and dear to my heart. A special shout-out to Helene Schulman and Karen Gilbert Johnston for their love and support.

To my family, for accepting me for who I am no matter what—you have my gratitude.

Thanks to all my teachers for their patience, truthfulness, guidance, and encouragement. Special thanks and gratitude to Diane Zimberhoff, David Hartman, Yvonne Christman, June Graham Spencer, Jim Spencer, Lisa Nichols and Loral Langemeir – you have shown me the way of inner freedom and continue to urge and support my walking toward it. Your teachings have greatly influenced my own work and are echoed in this book.

Thanks to all those who have shared their hearts with me as they courageously pursued being happy no matter what.

And a special thanks to Pam Popper for appreciating my work and joyously cheering me on.

# FOREWORD

So many of us have been suffering emotionally. Perhaps you've had the sadness of losses—of a parent, a friend, a pet—or unsuccessful relationships, too much alcohol, feelings of not being good enough or of unhappiness or of feeling ugly, or eating too much, not having enough money, physical ailments, unrelenting pain, anxiety or depression, or feeling lost and lonely…

An efficient way to alleviate this suffering is to break free from the overbearing feelings of being a victim. The roots of this victim consciousness are buried below the surface of your public self. Breaking free of this codependent, habitual thinking means recognizing these truths, rescinding blame, and owning your strengths. It requires that you become aware of limiting beliefs and attitudes operating within you that were developed as helpful aids during childhood, and now, as a result, reclaim your vital life force energy. What comes to your awareness is available to be reformed into the freedom of self-appreciation, self-care, and creativity.

I have been developing and refining programs on this topic for the past forty years. During this time, I committed myself to empower and propel the growth of healers who are dedicated to doing this work for themselves so that they can effectively bring this inner freedom to as many seekers of happiness on the planet as possible. The outcome is to move from dysfunction, disappointment, and perhaps even despair into a pleasing and productive life for individuals, as well as hope for healthy, progressive living for the community of all life on the planet.

It is from this experience that I wholeheartedly share with you the immense breadth of Ellen's reach as a beacon of light for so many in this regard. Ellen's thirty years as a life-solution strategist helping others, as well as living her own life as an artistic adventure, makes her an expert guide for your natural transformation from upset to joy.

As you read Be Happy No Matter What, Ellen walks you along a path that flows forward within yourself. Allow Ellen to show you a way to receive new information and how to consider it and absorb it easily. Let her walk you first through an understanding of how to find your center, then into a fine-arts appreciation of your life, and next to hear the whispers of your wise inner voice, and after that to decisions about whether or not to follow that voice. You'll reach a type of self-care that meets emotional needs within you that have never been met—until now. You will emerge with a new way of seeing yourself in your life. By presenting real-life examples and experiences, Ellen inspires and shows you how to see the ways a person can live through divorce and breast cancer surgery, for example, as adventure of the highest form.

In *Be Happy No Matter What*, Ellen provides you with a way out of feeling trapped within by feelings you dislike. She guides you to higher ground so you can get a new perspective on your troubles of today and those of long ago. While reading this book, negativity from the past and present are invited to be transformed so that you can fully enjoy life today. You can see yourself and your life anew. You have the opportunity to pleasingly find yourself and feel real freedom.

What's unique about this book is the way Ellen provides an enjoyable and soothing growth experience for the reader. She speaks in her calming voice as if the two of you are together in a quiet space. Her artistic way of using words creates gentle, self-healing experiences within you, the reader. And these experiences are attuned to your specific needs. *Be Happy No Matter What* is a guided tour of you, focusing on the rich meaning of your experiences, beliefs, thoughts, and attitudes. The reading reveals to you the previously overlooked rich value of your personal history, your self-appraisal, challenges you've encountered, and your unseen triumphs. This journey facilitates your movement through the doorway to your inner freedom.

I encourage you to allow the words in *Be Happy No Matter What* to flow in through your eyes on the pathway to your heart. Give yourself this gift of freedom to be happy no matter what. Your life is calling to you.

**Diane Zimberoff, LMFT**

Founder and Director, The Wellness Institute

Developer of Heart-Centered Hypnotherapy

Author of *Breaking Free from the Victim Trap*

and *Longing for Belonging*

www.wellness-institute.org

Issaquah, Washington, USA

June 2012

# CONTENTS

# Part IV
# Conclusion:

*Looking at Yourself through New Eyes*
## 223

# Part V
# Resources

# WELCOME

By picking up this book, you are taking the initiative to become truly free of inner upset.

There are many ways you may be feeling that inner upset. You may be in the midst of turmoil or at a crossroads in your life or have lost yourself along the way. You may be seeking better relationships and wish to communicate more clearly. Or you may desire to improve your home or business life, or need to hold others accountable. Or you may want to feel better emotionally and physically. Whether it is for one of these reasons or one that is entirely your own, you are ready for something that works for you and leads to being happy, no matter what.

As you read, you will find new thoughts and new perspectives just for your needs. Each of you reading the words unfolding here will be touched in ways that are designed specifically and perfectly for your unique growth and goals.

The mere reading of the words in this book is designed to take you along soothing paths of insight (also known as your *sight within*), through feelings of awakened accomplishment, into a rejuvenated and progressing sense of self-mastery, and on into the spaciousness of Inner Freedom.

In Part I, there is practical guidance on the concepts of **relaxing first** and **opening to allow** *Inner Freedom to* **unfold**, as well as setting the intention to *move at an* **easy pace**.

Then, in Part II, there are five self-valuing steps:

Step 1    Centering in My Self
Step 2    Appreciating Me and My Life as a Work of Art
Step 3    Hearing My Inner Wisdom
Step 4    Honoring My Self
Step 5    Caring for My Self

Through these five steps, or pathways, you can relax and then discover and access inner strengths and inner resources. By doing so, you will be poised to recognize and consistently access your own inner guidance. Having

traveled through the five steps to Inner Freedom, you
will then be ready to see how the *free you* interacts in
relationships and to see how differently the free you faces
life's challenging situations.

So now sit back, prepare to relax, and allow yourself to
proceed. This path has been made for your comfort
and ease.

PART I

# A New Kind of Preparation

## Relaxing First and Opening to Allow

As we get started, I want to introduce you to a few ideas that can serve you well at the beginning of any experience. Actually, they're helpful at any time, and for our purposes, they're introduced here to give you the best advantage as you use this material.

The idea of *relaxing first*, combined with *opening to allow*, clear space within you to focus on new information. They also give you the greatest ability to absorb this information.

So in order to prepare for what's to follow, each time you pick up *Be Happy No Matter What*, please allow yourself to relax into a chair, and then allow yourself to feel a wave of relaxation flow from the top of your head, taking with it any tension or tightness in your body and bringing with it ease, openness, and the feeling of *allowing* the relaxation as the wave moves all the way through your body and out your feet.

How about trying that now? I'll repeat the words:

Allow yourself to relax into a chair, and then allow

yourself to feel the wave of relaxation flow from the top of your head, moving down through your body and out through your feet. Feel the next wave of relaxation flow from the top of your head, this time taking with it any tension or tightness, down through your body and out through your feet. Feel the next wave of relaxation flow down from the top of your head, bringing with it ease that allows openness to flow all the way through your body.

That's great!

## Easily Moving Forward: Setting Your Pace

*Easily moving forward* and *setting an easy pace* consciously allows the words to wash into you, freeing you to experience their power. I have purposely written this book in short sections that allow you to slow the pace and absorb each section as well as giving you the ease of putting the book down and picking it up again where you left off.

For you to find your total Inner Freedom, I invite you to read the book as it's written. The content's sequence is to first build a foundation and then enhance your self-knowledge and finally your ability to use it. After you have finished this book, you will likely return to various chapters at different times.

No worries!

Along the way, I will help you with relaxing, allowing, and easy pacing.

# 5 Steps to Inner Freedom

## An Introduction and Some Basics.

Many if not all of you have inner upsets about big things, small things, and subtle things. Many people believe that changing one's situation or the people in their lives is the best way to solve one's inner upset. Our society implies and suggests that acquiring things and money are also avenues to happiness. Get a new job, get a new partner, move somewhere else—are you familiar with this approach? While you might get some temporary relief, after the quick-fix effect wears off, most of us would most likely resume endless attempts to alleviate our inner upset by changing our outer circumstances.

Instead, I'm going to show you how to listen to your inner truths and to focus on what you need in order to achieve true and lasting Inner Freedom and happiness no matter what.

**_Inner upset can actually be used
as a guide to Inner Freedom._**

This is the beginning of seeing things in a new way and experiencing the truths needed for inner health and a happy outlook.

One truth is this: The upset felt in a current situation is echoing upsets from earlier in life. The upset is already in you and is simply being triggered by something in your current situation.

Here's an example:

Recall a time when you were upset that someone was impatient with you or hurrying you along. Were you able to calmly say, "Oh, listen, I see you are in a hurry. Why don't you go ahead without me and I'll be along shortly," or did you instead feel upset rising up inside you, or even flashing instantly, as if the person was doing something terrible to you? Was your upset much more than the situation actually called for?

Something triggered feelings inside of you that ran deeper than what was called for by the current situation. This happens to everyone until they realize this truth:

11

**_No matter how much you change what's outside of you, you take yourself and your trigger-ready sensitivities with you wherever you go._**

And guess what? All your perceptions and ideas go with you too.

You picked up this book because, on some level, you've realized that the capacity to change your experience is within you. The task can actually become teasing out what you don't like that's going on today from what might be your projection of what happened in the past. And even if you haven't felt like taking full charge of your life, you have been working your way to consider this as at least a possibility. You might even have had fear about taking full charge or believed you can't.

However, all self-reflection and your self-work up through now have led you to this point of willingness to discover this capacity to change.

Take a breath.

I'm here to tell you that this is easier than you think.

After all, you have already lived through many challenging episodes in the grand story of your life. We all have!

From your very beginnings—even before you could speak—you've witnessed innumerable things. Clients have told me they recall what was going on in the womb and even before. This is actually true for all of us. You too had awarenesses before you could speak, and just no way to express them. You were too small, literally, and didn't have the language. If you could have taken charge, then you would have. It's true that little ones have clarity, but when we are little, adults have power over us. Through no fault of our own small size, we have no language, no authority—we just don't have what it takes to take charge. (If this topic interests you, read some of the works of Michael Newton.)

Even these days, when so much is known about the awareness and sensitivity of children, many people disregard the fact that babies have awareness and thoughts. Babies and children (even teenagers and young adults) are treated as if they couldn't possibly have any sense of what's best for their own lives.

So it's no wonder so many of us feel like we are trapped victims or pawns under the control of those around us, such as our parents, spouses, partners, and bullying employers, as well as self-righteous, entitled, helpless, and unhappy coworkers and employees.

This book offers you an easy and soothing way to play with the idea that

**no matter what, inside of yourself,
you can be and feel truly happy and free.**

I encourage you to play with the idea that you are the author of your life—even if it feels impossible that you could be. Among the many great things that can grow out of this concept of authorship is the really useful idea that *you* have the *author*-ity in your life. Even if you choose to collaborate with coauthors, you have the sole authority over you. This means that other people's opinions, while maybe interesting, truly hold no weight.

I want you to really consider the following, whether you believe it or not:

You are due acknowledgement for the hard work you've done on yourself for years, whether you are conscious of this work or not. It's not possible for you to be where you are in your life if this were not so. It's not been easy to get to where you are in life. You have forged through the challenges of your childhood, teen years, and early adult life, through relationships, through a variety of mid-life realizations, and through many ideas about yourself, others, and life.

The ups and downs of life have not stopped you. They may have dragged you down, or they might even have propelled you forward. Yet you continue to seek information, techniques, new approaches, and a clearer understanding so you can make your life better and help yourself feel better. Your openness has allowed you to take in improvements. You have learned so many lessons.

And now you're here. You got here—hooray!—to the doorway of your Inner Freedom. (Do you see the soft smile on my face?) You are now up to allowing your Inner Freedom to finally seep out, gently saturating the layers of your being.

Take a breath and rest here a moment before going on. Rest with these thoughts.

## Inner Freedom is a reality.

Hmm…Inner Freedom. That sounds so good. But is it really possible? To experience lasting Inner Freedom?

Well, why not? It's been written that what you think becomes real and what you believe becomes so. Personally, I've found this to be true. *There are ways to give yourself the inner experiences you'd like.*

What if I tell you the following is true? *Inner Freedom is already inside you, waiting for you to touch it.* Are you open to considering this?

If you are, I'm here to support you stepping into your Inner Freedom. This book provides tips and information and new twists to add to what you already know.

As you read more, I'll invite you to consider new thoughts that are designed to free you inside. Be aware that some of the thoughts may feel upside down or odd, so please be sensitive to yourself. Notice if you feel like shying away. If that's the case, it may be wise to try on the ideas before prematurely casting them aside. You need only consider the ideas—there's no need to agree with or adopt them—in order for you to get the benefits. And you can do this in the privacy of yourself.

**Talk to me about your challenges.**

Before we go any further, tell me some of what you are facing in your life today. If we were together in my office, I'd be asking you to tell me about the following items, so instead, please make a check mark beside the ones that apply to you.

- ☐ My body hurts
- ☐ I don't have enough time in the day to do all I set out to do
- ☐ I never feel like I'm doing enough
- ☐ I feel depressed

- ☐ My hormones drive me wild
- ☐ I have headaches
- ☐ My children require so much attention that I'm drained
- ☐ My husband requires so much attention, yet attending to the kids is already more than enough
- ☐ My husband and I don't really connect
- ☐ My mother irritates me (she can be alive or have passed on)
- ☐ The criticisms of my father haunt me (he can be alive or have passed on)
- ☐ The criticisms of my mother haunt me (she can be alive or have passed on)
- ☐ I say things to my children that I don't even mean
- ☐ I have made my business successful, yet I still have no time for myself
- ☐ I have made my business and family life successful, yet I'm still disgruntled and not happy
- ☐ I feel that at this time in my life I should be joyful and happy—and I'm not
- ☐ I'm tired of my job
- ☐ I'm a super coordinator and need a break
- ☐ I haven't had a vacation in years
- ☐ I take vacations and can't seem to relax

- [ ] I feel like I'm on automatic, going through the motions of daily responsibilities

- [ ] I still have panic attacks

- [ ] I still have anxiety

- [ ] I have a hard time getting people to do what I need them to do

- [ ] People expect too much of me

- [ ] No one in my family really understands me

- [ ] I'm really on my own

- [ ] I'm not having any fun

- [ ] I practice Self-Care (e.g., I go the gym, I get my nails done, I take relaxing baths and even go on vacations), yet I still feel miserable

- [ ] I feel like I'm on a treadmill going nowhere in life

- [ ] I don't get a solid night's sleep

- [ ] I want to eat nutritiously but there's no time

- [ ] I eat on the run (even if it's nutritious)

- [ ] I'm getting older and it's bothering me

- [ ] I take great care of all those around me, but when will someone take care of me?

- [ ] I work so hard. Will it ever let up?

- [ ] Sometimes I feel like crying, but I'm afraid to start because I may not be able to stop

- [ ] It's all on my shoulders

- ☐ I seem to be able to say all the right things to other people, and I know I've grown a great deal, yet I still feel awful

- ☐ I have no time to try new things, spend time with friends, or really enjoy myself

- ☐ I can't seem to lose the weight I want to lose, no matter what I do

- ☐ I can't seem to gain the weight I want to gain, no matter what I do

- ☐ No matter how I fix myself up on the outside, I feel so awful on the inside

**I feel stuck in:**

- ☐ My job

- ☐ My primary relationship

My habits of:

- ☐ Negative thinking

- ☐ Eating (overeating, undereating, binging, purging, eating junk food)

- ☐ Drinking

- ☐ Smoking

- ☐ Caffeine use

- ☐ Prescription drug use

- ☐ Non-prescription drug use

- ☐ Excessive exercise

- [ ] I'm irritable for no reason
- [ ] I'm angry for no reason
- [ ] I'm excessively angry
- [ ] I'm excessively sad
- [ ] I'm confused about what to do in my life
- [ ] I wonder what my purpose is
- [ ] I'm not passionate about anything
- [ ] I feel like crying for no reason
- [ ] I feel like crying and yet I just can't
- [ ] I want to make the most out of the rest of my life but don't know how

By now, you might be wondering, "How could I possibly be so close to my Inner Freedom when so much of what I face still feels so insurmountable?"

But remember that personal growth is not linear. It's not along a straight line, as we have been taught to logically expect things that progress to be. Because so much of what human beings are about is actually outside of our awareness (93 percent is in the subconscious mind, while only 7 percent is in the conscious mind or what we are aware of), this leaves only small pieces of the grand pie that are visible to us. So basing conclusions and judgments (and worries) about your personal growth on only parts of the total picture gives you an inaccurate sense of what is occurring. You never know when a realization is just around the corner and it will spring you light-years ahead. Thus, it's best to keep an open mind here, for maximum self-respect.

## Tapping into your trapped energy.

As you clear out the final dust bunnies in the corners of growth, you may encounter traces of issues you've already overcome. When you sweep away these last vestiges of troublesomeness, you extract any of your energy still trapped there. That energy is considered by many to be your precious life force energy. Some people enjoy anticipating the reclaiming of this energy. If this thought feels comfortable, you don't have to wait. Go ahead and start the process, and enjoy the anticipation.

But the rest of you might be wondering what *clearing and sweeping away* actually means.

Here's how it works: Through a gentle process of considering some new thoughts, you'll find that those old beliefs, ideas, conclusions, and decisions—whatever no longer serves you—fall away. You become unblocked and you feel your energy starting to flow, maybe for the first time. This is your energy that may have been stopped up since much earlier times. You may find you have a new curiousness about things and will want to look into them a little deeper. Many people I've worked with have found treasures of self-realization when they've more closely examined areas they'd already discovered. Of course, this is not required in order to receive the benefits in store for you. Keep asking what *clearing and sweeping away* actually mean for you.

## Exploring the benefits of Inner Freedom.

Ah, Inner...inner relaxation. But what is it, exactly?

It's many things: No rushing. Plenty of trust that what is happening in your life is exactly what is supposed to be happening at this time and is in your best interest (and is, coincidentally, in the best interests of those around you).

It's an inner knowing that makes you confident about your choices, so no more second guessing, no more guilt. It's feeling that time is irrelevant and that you are fulfilling your purpose even if it's not totally clear what that purpose is. It's having faith in others to make the wisest decisions for their own highest good at a given moment (even if you can't see any wisdom in their decisions, behavior, or ways). It's recognizing that others' opinions about you are truly none of your business, no matter how verbal those other people are. It's trusting your own inner knowing about which direction to take, and knowing—without a doubt—that the process of trial and error is a great avenue of self-satisfaction for the experimenter in you. Inner Freedom is experiencing your life as an interesting adventure with wonderful surprises at every turn. It's knowing peace in your heart, and feeling that all weights have been lifted off your shoulders and back, and there's no more tightness in your stomach. It's clearheadedness and lightheartedness. It's liking who you are, who you are with, and what you are doing. And it's so much more.

To ensure that you are open to receiving new

information, do this simple exercise, first with your eyes open and then again with your eyes closed.

## Inviting you to...
# Do This Now

Bending both arms at the elbows, hold your hands out in front of you, palms up.

Tighten both fists as much as you can. Tighten your whole body as you do this.

Feel the feeling of **closed**.

Now slowly open your hands. Feel your whole body open.

Feel the feeling of **openness**.

Do this exercise one more time with your eyes closed.

Now you've got it. And you can also use this as an easy way to relax during the day.

I invite you to put this book down, relax, breathe, and allow the meaning and energy of the words to settle into you, flow through you, become yours. When you return, you'll pick this book up again, refreshed, relaxed, and ready and open to receive *new* information supporting your flowing forward.

# CHAPTER ONE

## Step 1:
## Centering in My Self

### Each Person Is Their Own Center

Get ready for some new ideas to try on.

Here's the first one:

**You are the star
in your life.**

I could swear I heard you say, "What?"

No one's ever mentioned this idea, right?

Okay, take a moment and B R E A T H E . And think about it this way:

You are in the center of you, and you're the only person who is looking out through your eyes. Your life actually revolves around you, all 360 degrees.

Now imagine that you are the sun, and the solar system represents some aspects of your life. Can you see now, how your life revolves around you? This is true even if you have intended to devote your life to others.

No one else but you can have the experiences you are having. No one else but you can see your experience in the exact way that you do. That's a fact.

This is one of the many forms of uniqueness that exists.

## I am the main star in my life.

Before we go on, I want you to really feel the meaning of the words, "I am the main star in my life." It's okay to use your imagination if you have to, or even to play pretend. Close your eyes until you can see only the words, "I am the main star in my life," in front of you. Allow yourself to try on the feeling of being the star in your life.

Now picture this. You get up in the morning and already you have many things on your mind: getting the children off to school, seeing your husband off for the day, preparing to run errands, and heading to work. Everything that you are focusing on revolves around you. Nothing in your life happens without you. You initiate every action and your part of every interaction in your life. You are the entity that makes the people and situations in your world run smoothly for you. You are the center star in your life and they are revolving around you.

Take as much time as you need to experience this concept. Once you can imagine your world revolving around you, let that feeling infuse the air around you.

As you breathe, B R E A T H E in the feeling of being the star in your life. Let the feeling fill your lungs. Take another relaxing breath and this time, *sense* the feeling of you being the star in your life, and let it flow out from your lungs and into your bloodstream. Sense the energy of this new idea nourishing all your muscles, nerves, bones, organs, and systems in your body. Allow the nourishing to go deeply into your cells. Take another breath and this time, as you exhale, allow all the tension, tightness, and doubt to flow out with your breath.

It's time to anchor in this very positive way of looking out through your eyes. Let a color come to you (no thinking here—just allow any color to come to you) that further enhances this experience. If no color comes to you, imagine one.

Now, as if you could, breathe that color up through the soles of your feet, allowing the color to saturate every cell of your body.

Good, you are doing great.

Relax here a few moments.

Or even close this book for

a while in order to open up

the space to absorb this new

thought for consideration.


BREATHE

## ❧ WELCOME BACK

Now that you have anchored in this new thought, "I am the star in my life," I want to share how our environment challenges your holding onto your center. Let's take a look at what the rest of the world thinks about this thought and how their thinking has affected you.

Have you ever been put down and criticized by your elders, relatives, loved ones, friends, brave teenage children, business associates, or even yourself? Did it take the form of "The whole world revolves around you!" as if it's a bad thing? What about "Who do you think you are? Do you think the whole world revolves around you?" Or maybe it took the form of "You are so self-centered!" or even "You are so self-centered, just like a child."

There! They've spotted the truth. What they don't realize is that it's true for them too. And, of course, it's not something to criticize you for, or to be mean about.

Now, back to the part about being self-centered like a child—yet another truth!

As a child, you *naturally* started out by approaching the world from a centered perspective. In fact, when you were a baby, you thought everything was an extension of you, and any book on human development discusses this. As a baby, it's hard to tell the difference between what is me and what is something else.

Very early on, you came to believe (from the smiles and frowns of the adults who cared for you) that you made the people around you happy or unhappy. You concluded that their facial expressions and the sounds of their verbal responses in reaction to you were proof of this. This was the beginning of you thinking you are responsible for other people's feelings, and that somehow your world revolves around them, and that your actions are defined by what they think of you. You didn't have the knowledge back then that they were entities unto themselves. They were responsible for their feelings and actions and you likewise are responsible for yours.

The adults may even have said things like, "Make Mommy happy, eat," or "Don't make me mad, or I'll send you to your room," or "Eat all your vegetables so you don't make Mommy sad," or "You hurt my feelings," or "If Daddy hears you say that, he'll have a heart attack!" or "Be quiet, or you'll upset Daddy/Grandma/Grandpa/me."

And so, many people have unconsciously gone on to become people pleasers.

Later you learned your parents' responses to your report card, to you coming home late, to doing or not doing your homework, etc. It became easy to anticipate how others would react to you.

In fact, most everything in our environment reinforces the overrated value of the opinion of others. The public-school grading system is an example that many people have been subjected to. Competition with others is another example. And what about all the times adults have given the impression to children that they need to behave a certain way, or else! Not only is the message communicating that your behavior adversely affects others, but it's also clearly stating that you will be punished, put down, degraded, shamed, or bullied into submission.

*Inviting you to...*
# Do This Now

First, take a breath and
feel yourself relax.

Take another breath
and relax even more.

Now, in the privacy of yourself,
set the intention to be honest.
Not for anyone else—just for you.

One more breath…

Now, on a scale from one to ten, to what degree have you ever given thought to what someone else thinks about you? For many of us, it's very often at least an eight.

Experiencing this over and over and over again for years and years has become a conditioned response and has pulled you out of your natural center!

The reverse is also true. You latched onto the idea that other people are responsible for your feelings. Kids blame others or themselves when they are upset. Have you ever heard yourself think or actually say, "You made me feel, mad/sad/lonely/guilty"? The adults around you taught you this idea of who is responsible for what. Unfortunately, there's nothing in society or in our conversations that lead us to conclude otherwise.

Believing this since you were little and basing your actions, behavior, and self talk on these ideas has reinforced this pattern into a fairly deep groove, called an *energy grove*. Not only have you become conditioned to hold others responsible for *making you* feel bad, with all the associated resentment, anger, disgust, rebelling—passive or active—punitiveness, and whatever else you've got in there, you also hold others responsible for making you happy.

That's why so many people are eager (and at times desperate) to find particular types of partners who they mistakenly believe will make them happy. They are afraid that they will be miserable on their own, thinking that they need someone else to *make them* happy. When you believe you need someone else to make you happy, you may be a person who has given away credit for your natural, birthright-centered feelings. That's what you are doing when you seek your happiness solely at the hands of others.

But no worries! One of the blessings of your shift to recognize that you are the owner of your feelings is that you don't have to wait for others to "correct" a situation. In fact, it's not in their jurisdiction. It's only doable by you. This is not difficult when you understand and set clear intentions. (I'll talk about *intention* later in the book.)

Believing that your happiness is caused by others' words and behavior is *a **faulty thought**.*

This thought can be changed, however. In truth, your happiness is your own and its *emergence*—not its *creation*—can be triggered by another's words and behavior. Your feelings are yours and you have a full complement of them which you are entitled to feel to the hilt. You can later learn to modulate your feelings *as you desire*—a new thought to consider. You can even reach a point where you select the feeling you want to experience. When my teacher said this to me, I thought it was ridiculous. But guess what? It's doable. Will you decide to choose your feelings?

How are you doing so far? You've taken in quite a bit by this point.

Let's stop here a moment
to breathe and relax.

a h h h h !

*Inviting you to...*
# Do This Now

Take another breath in slowly
and, while exhaling, allow any
pent-up tension and tightness to
just fall away from your body.

Let it drift away.

See it drift away, float away,
leave you.

You are doing great.

You have so much courage. Not everyone brings themselves to new ideas. Not everyone allows their general concept of life to be shaken up in order to grow. Imagine a standing ovation for you, the **star in your life**. Go slowly with this. Imagine it in full color with full feelings. If you are shy about taking this in, or minimizing this opportunity, it means go slower, open more to receiving this new experience.

I'm encouraging you to do this because it has a cleansing, recuperating, uplifting, and freeing effect. Remember that's why you picked up this book. Take as much time as you need.

BREATHE

Ready to go on?

**Retain credit for your feelings.**

This is true for the ones you like and the ones you don't like.

Giving others credit, responsibility, or blame for your feelings gives away your precious personal assertiveness and power. This is actually your life-force energy. Even reading only the above statement, and considering it, moves you into position to reclaim that lost personal power—your precious life-force energy.

You were taught to like certain feelings and to dislike others, but there is merit in appreciating all your feelings. You were too young to realize that you were giving away your power when you believed your happiness or unhappiness relied on others.

Some of you may want to get nurturing-type help with retrieving your power by *valuing all* your feelings. As you learn to do this, it gets easier to take credit for them all, even the ones you don't like.

Here are several examples: One feeling you might choose to avoid is disappointment. Who likes to experience disappointment? Nobody. However, if you look at disappointment from another angle, you can see it from a different perspective. A friend of mine once triggered deep disappointment in me when she repeatedly canceled our appointments. She realized I was disappointed and asked me about it. My first reaction was to deny this, but she pushed forward, having realized how truly disappointed I was. She explained to me that my disappointment was a sign of how much she meant to me. She thanked me. I was amazed. That's when I began to value this feeling that previously I had hated.

Another example is having trouble saying no, whether you need to do so because of a lack of time or a dislike for the task. Or maybe you worry about insulting or possibly hurting the other person's feelings. Once you realize your saying no actually allows the other person to make their best decision for themselves, you are freeing yourself and them.

When you allow yourself to see all your feelings with the benefits they bring, then you are able to have more freedom to play with different interactions and different situations, even ones you dislike. The previous examples offer ways to start looking at your own reactions in order to appreciate your feelings and the deeper meanings within yourself.

If you are interested in an additional resource on owning your feelings, there is a great book by two early teachers of mine, June and Jim Spencer, called *No Bad Feelings*. My copy was published in Colorado by the Let Go & Live Institute Ltd. in 2002. The book is now out of print but it is still available at various sites on the Internet. The words in the Spencers' book enable you to value *all* your feelings in a very nurturing way.

How about taking a break
here to digest what you've
taken in, and then come
back a bit later for more.


Remember to

BREATHE

## ∽ WELCOME BACK

**You are the sole choice-maker.**

Now that you know your feelings originate within you,
we can get back to looking at you as the leading star of
your life in order to consider several additional thoughts.

As the star, you are the only one who can win the starring role award at the Academy Awards. Everyone else
in your life is a supporting actor—even if they don't act
supportively! They can only get the best-supporting-role
award. Remember, Shakespeare said, "All the world's a
stage and all the people are players."

Now, that's true for everyone. Everyone you meet is the
main star in his or her life.

How does that feel to you? Is that upsetting or relieving?
If you are a mom who needs to coordinate and direct
the lives of her children, you are the supervisor—not the
star—of those lives. It's wise for the child's healthy development to have you in a strong, supportive character

role and not a mom demanding the starring role. If you are anguished by a loved one not listening to your expert direction to seek the help of a doctor, lawyer, Shaman, or therapist, it can be a relief to realize that this person is the star in his or her own life. You can let go of control over that person's life and yet still give plenty of support—that's the fullness of your role.

You may discover here that control has been a huge issue for your character's role. See what it will take for you to *let go* of any fantasy in which you have more influence than your character can truly be responsible for.

Do you need help with this idea? If so, keep reading, because help is on the way! The next new thought will assist you with this concept.

Think about this: There are multiple movies all going on at once in your life right now. It can be confusing until you own which character you have control over. Remember, you are the central star in only your life, and you are in supporting roles to others in their movies.

Now, those of you who aim to devote yourself to a life of service to others may challenge this perspective. I see no conflict here because even if you choose a life of devotion to others, you are the one making this life choice and as such you are still the star in only your movie.

Accepting that you are the sole choice-maker in your life leads you directly to **Inner Freedom**. Acknowledging this truth alleviates the negative self-judgment that you are supposed to be something you are not—the controller in someone else's life. The benefit of the "you are the star in your life" idea is applying it (*thinking* it) to counter thoughts of negative self-judgment. The immediate effect this has is to dissolve the negative thought that you are telling yourself about you (the self-judgment). As you hear yourself say, "I'm the star in my life," over and over again, it begins to take hold and becomes a default setting upon which many wonderful ideas about yourself can grow. An example is thinking to yourself that you have so much on your shoulders as you supervise the lives of others. Yet as you practice recognizing that you are the star in your life (not in theirs), something about the burden lifts.

You stand taller as you realize, "this is *my* movie." In your mind, you shift the dynamics among the players on your stage, and then you also see how to better play your supportive roles in other people's scenarios. There are lots of experiences that can come of this new thinking. Let yourself play with this idea. You can simply contemplate it for a while. And then, when you are ready, move on to the next page.

# Inviting you to...
# Do This Now

Take out a piece of blank paper and title it, "I Am the Star of My Life." List four situations you are in now, four you were in in the past, and four you would like to be in in the future. Whatever comes to mind is exactly perfect for this experience.

Now, note next to each entry how seeing yourself as the star in your life and seeing the other people in these situations as the stars of their own lives improves your thinking about these experiences. Notice how your feelings change in response to these situations, now that you see who's who in the cast.

Take as much time as you need to do this in a way that is easy and soothing.

Now that we have discussed you being the star of your life and your supporting roles in other people's lives, you may be feeling a little self-centered. Good!

The self-centered criticisms are my favorites, and I like to counter them with such responses as:

> People seek therapy in order to *become* centered.
>
> People learn meditation to *become* centered.
>
> Counting yourself down from an angry peak is also a form of centering.

So when you hear these criticisms from others or from yourself, remember: *centered* is a good thing.

A final thought before we move on to the next chapter:

There are many limiting beliefs that come only from within. No one can give you a feeling—you are solely responsible for your feelings. Here are a few that you may have experienced:

*I'm a victim*

*I'm to blame*

*I'm so discouraged*

*I'm down in the dumps*

*I'm disappointed*

*I'm depleted of energy*

*I'm frustrated*

*I'm downright angry*

You have survived your childhood, which is where many of these feelings originated. The good news is that, as you journey through the rest of this book, you will learn that these feelings are within your control and are *not* controlled by your environment, your family, your job, and not even your childhood.

**Your feelings reside within you and can only be invited up by your view of what's happening. This means that the reaction you have to someone else's comments comes from within you, from your feelings about yourself.**

*Everything is in the eye of the beholder. Everything!*

CHAPTER TWO

# Step 2:
# Appreciating Me and
# My Life as a Work of Art

## Portrait and Landscape

The world provides lots of triggers for us to feel unhappy. It's easy to have our minds be marauded by the troubles we experience in our lives and what we witness going on for others too. We are bombarded daily with news of misery, violence, and economic downturn. Every seven minutes, television commercials repeat, either subliminally or outright entraining our minds—and those of our children—with intense, visual images of depression. (Well, that and the desirability for men to improve their sexual functioning with the use of drugs!) Much of what's on television is a wellspring of tension and anxiety: businesses relentlessly press us to purchase their products, and the shows and movies are overwhelmingly crime-laden and dark, with violent images that bombard our brains—our mental computers.

Many of us have been trained to see life and ourselves through the lenses given to us by society: the news-reporting and communications industries, the Food and Drug Administration, food-related councils, the pharmaceutical industry, exclusionary religious groups, political groups, business monopolies, the companies and professions we work for, narrow-minded parents…the list goes on.

Wow, that reality is pretty heavy. It weighs on us daily, and without us consciously registering its effects on our psyches.

But there *is* a way for you to counteract the negative effects of our environment and to *totally shift your energy to*—to infuse yourself with—health, happiness, and joy.

Even in the midst of the chaos we experience around

us, many people still set the intention to Be Happy No Matter What. Self-appreciation and finding what there is to love about life are direct approaches with constructive, productive, and permanent outcomes.

## Set the intention to see what else is out there.

An extreme, dramatic, and effective way to counteract the magnetic pull of the doldrums is to set the intention to see what else exists in each moment besides the destructive messages of limitations and the emotional-bummer energies. Once that intention is set, what follows next is truly amazing. Constructive (i.e., the antithesis of what we were experiencing) ideas begin to reveal themselves. And then the energy of these new, productive ideas supplants the stale, limiting, downing, and depressing understanding of life that society has had us operating under. The result is breathing sighs of relief while looking at yourself and realizing that the "inside you" is okay and safe in the midst of your challenging and daily situations. These new thoughts now position you to view yourself and others in the highest possible light.

Yes, changing one's thinking—one's orientation to life—to self-appreciation is a radical approach, and you might think that it's very hard work. No worries. You've already accomplished hard work in your life. Actually, living under the negative bombardment of institutions and people is the hardest work of all. So deciding to choose a lighter path is easy by comparison.

And there's something else. Something of a very helpful nature is going on, energetically speaking, these days.

Let's look at it this way: Adopting a self-appreciative view means you're clearing away what's been in the way—negativity. It won't be the hard work that it's been in the past. Now, it's as if you are getting helpful boosts of clearing energy from the cosmos. You're open to receiving that energy now because you have a sincere intention, a willing heart, and a developing faith in your progress with each step forward. These are the ingredients that forge your way out of the negativity of this world and into your Inner Freedom, and, ultimately, to Being Happy No Matter What.

# The art of appreciating me.

Take a moment now and relax your body.

Call the energy of calm and relaxation into the room you're in. Let the air become infused with calm.

Now, breathe in this relaxation and calm, allowing them to fill your lungs, travel out into your blood, and nourish every cell, molecule, and atom of every part and particle of your being.

Calm, calm throughout.

ahhhh!

Rest a moment here in your
calm and feel your relaxing openness…

Take as much time as you need.

Now, in your openness, allow
the following two ideas to wash
through you:

## 1. Appreciating Me and
## My Life as a Work of Art

Have you ever thought of your life
as a work of art?

Take a moment and let this first idea
settle in. And when you are ready, go
on and add the second idea.

## 2. Appreciating Me, All Aspects of Me

Think about when you look at a
work of art. A painting, let's say.
What do you notice about it?

**Let's start with the colors**

The tone of the colors?

The hue of the colors?

How are the colors used?

**The medium**

Oils?

Watercolors?

Chalk?

Pencil?

Multi-media?

**The depth in the portrayal**

The foreground?

The background?

**Is movement implied or portrayed?**

**The types and textures of stroke marks**

Pallet knife strokes, brushstrokes?

Smooth or textured?

**The artist's style?**

**Your sense of what the artist is communicating?**

**What you get and experience as you view the work of art?**

**The expanse of the portrayal?**

**Are there discrete segments in the portrayal?**

**Is it abstract?**

**Is it concrete?**

**What about interpretation?**

**Are the lines clear or vague, firm or soft?**

**Can you detect**
  Contrast?
  Brightness?
  Dullness?
  Expansiveness?
  Narrowness?

**What are the relative sizes portrayed?**

**Do you see people and/or animals?**

What are they doing?

What are their facial expressions?

What do they seem to be saying?
(use your imagination here, make
believe you can hear them speaking)

**Are there shadows?**

**How is shadow used?**

**Are there plants?**

**Is there a sense of movement in the painting?**

**How does what you see affect you?**

**What feelings are evoked?**

**If the artwork happens to be music, are you able to notice and appreciate some of these traits:**

Speed or tempo: fast, slow, or a combination?

Tone?

Pitch?

Softness and/or loudness?

Jaggedness and/or smoothness?

Erratic feelings or those of calmness?

Mellowness and/or brashness?

Expansiveness?

Pointedness?

Echoes?

Reverberations and/or vibrations?

Are there pauses and silence mixed into the music?

Is it familiar or strange to your ear?

How does this piece of music affect you?

What feelings does it evoke?

## Masterpieces defy comparison.

It's generally easy to remember that appreciating art is subjective. Each person appreciating a single piece of artwork will have his or her own way of viewing it and valuing it. And, actually, each piece of art has so many aspects that artwork defies comparison.

Keep this in mind whenever you compare yourself to someone else. You, yourself, or people you know may have been plagued with or have had bouts of negative self-judgment. It can be detected in negative self-talk, in negative thoughts repeated in your head, or any downing or demeaning conclusions about yourself.

*Allowing yourself to see yourself and your life as an artistic masterpiece instantly dispels negative self-judgment. Permanently adopting this approach will eliminate self-judgement and the habit of comparing yourself and your life to others. Consider adopting this way of viewing yourself and your life. You'll feel better right away.*

Sit quietly and try this thought on for size:

*"I am a unique, artistic masterpiece."*

You don't have to buy into this thought; it's not for sale.
Just try it on. If it feels uncomfortable, no worries. You
can try it on later and see how it fits then. If you like
something about how it feels, stay with it and allow it to
grow within you.

ALLOW

Okay, let's go on.

**My life is a live portrayal of all the scenes of my life.**

Here's another lens through which to gain discerning appreciation:

There is a philosophy that suggests that you are the author, actor, director—even the casting director—and the viewer of your life. If you take this on as "all my upset is all my fault," then you are viewing this idea with negative self-judgment, and that can be unsettling. If that's what comes up for you, I ask you to put that thought on a nice, safe cushion and set it aside for now. We will deal with it later. (Take whatever time you need to see, sense, or feel yourself laying that negative thought aside for the time being. If you need to, return to breathing. Take a moment to calm and relax yourself.)

Let's imagine that your life is a really great film with lots of human-interest aspects. It has or has had high drama, plenty of emotional scenes, booms and busts, and perhaps some gut-wrenching scenes. You may have loved and lost or never loved at all. There's probably been some high adventure, even life and death struggles, and certainly intense grief and loss, high hopes and disappointed expectations, achievements, struggles, low points, and hard-won high points.

The approach that you are the writer, director, actor, etc., of your epic film has some great benefits. It means that you have the authority (as the author) to alter and improve your script, to choose different players, and to view the scenes from different angles. Basically, the changes needed for you to experience joy in place of upset.

### *Thus, the joy or upset you experience is 100 percent under your jurisdiction.*

Ahhhh. Now you see there's no need to believe that your relief, happiness, or joy relies on other people changing. Looking for, waiting for, and insisting that others change their behavior, beliefs, and feelings is not necessary. Looking for others to change is really like going to a dry well for water; it drains your precious energy. It's true, of course, that one can get temporary relief when others change. And occasionally people do change, and that's a nice bonus. But its effect cannot be anchored or rooted into your self. It's not one of your tools in your inner toolbox, so you cannot count on it.

In this respect, the effect is from outside of you and therefore not yours to own. On the other hand, you can really make something of your own of lasting usefulness, by working from the inside of you outward, rather than from the outside of you inward.

I'm not saying to turn away from the benefits of the changes others bring about in themselves. What I'm saying is that an efficient and effective application of your energy (in the service of your emotional health) is to **embrace ownership of your own experience**. It brings fuller, lasting, and permanent relief to realize that you have what you need within yourself to remedy your upsets. You don't need to wait or rely on the actions of others for your upset to be remedied. Even if you don't know exactly how to access what is within yourself, your intention to discover and your expanding self-awareness will reveal exactly what you need from within yourself.

I'm all about encouraging you to enjoy what *is,* and at the same time capitalizing on the effectiveness of certain thoughts and understandings that are available for you to discover and use *in the future* to facilitate and comfortably accelerate your own growth. Whatever is within your purview is yours to make the most of and capitalize upon.

This is a good place for some relaxed breathing.

Think of bringing the energy of relaxation and calm into the room. As you do so, close your fists as tightly as you can and hold that tightness for a few seconds.

Now, open both your hands and feel the letting go of the tightness.

Do it a second time. Tighten both fists and this time when you open them, breathe a big sigh of relief. Pretend that this feeling of relief and ease is an easy chair. Nestle in and get cozy.

From this coziness, and with a really light approach, let these words just float into your consciousness.

## *"My life is a really great film."*

Imagine what this film looks like. Allow yourself to see its beginning, how it has unfolded, and what purview is yours to leverage and use. Gather the information you have learned thus far, such as the concept of My Life is a Work of Art, and visualize the scenes with new eyes.

As you view these scenes, be aware that you can slow things down to get a better look. Imagine that somewhere inside of you is a speed-control dial that you can access to slow things down to get a better appreciation of the details in each moment.

We live in a very fast-paced environment. Have you ever felt that time is going by too rapidly? Have you ever taken pride in multi-tasking and making the most use of fleeting time? As a passenger in a car, have you ever noticed that it's very difficult to see much detail as the scenery whizzes by? If you've experienced any of this, take note! This is good information. It says, "slow things down so that you can appreciate the details and nuances of your life." It's the same for your really great film. You don't have to miss a minute of your life.

In fact, each moment is a precious gift. Sometimes it's hidden and takes appreciation to reveal it. You can open these gifts at any time. Even moments past, that have gone unexperienced or unappreciated, can be reviewed and recovered.

## Inviting you to...
# Do This Now

In your mind, bring up one of your favorite episodes in your life.

Now, play with the speed-control dial.

Slowly review one of your favorite parts of that episode. Now, fast forward to another part later on. See how this works?

To gain appreciation of yourself, your life, and of others, do this with your life situations while they are happening. (It might take you several times to get the hang of this.)

Here's how: As quickly as something needs to take place right now, you can play with the speed-control dial and slow the action down in your perception (which is 100 percent in your control) to take a closer look at what's actually happening. It's like looking closely at a work of art. You can even say out loud, "Whoa, let's all slow down here," to the people around you, which will change the speed of the concrete experience as well. Of course, if you are in an emergency situation, you may just want to slow down your experiencing and not your physical actions.

Can you see how your experience of a situation can be treated separately from the other things going on in the situation?

Play with the dial adjusting the speed at which you experience what's happening around you; the speed with which you enjoy things; the speed with which you react or respond to your own feelings, the behavior of others, and of what's asked of you; the speed of your eating; the speed of your hearing or listening to others; the speed at which you accomplish tasks. All of these speeds can be adjusted consciously with intention, i.e., with your speed-control dial.

You now know about the speed-control dial. It is available in your inner toolbox anytime you want it.

You have probably heard the expressions "Stop and smell the roses" or "Wake up and smell the coffee." That's what you are learning how to do here.

It is part of your birthright to experience all the beauty there is to experience in this life. In fact, it is present now and you only need to adjust the speed to focus on the beauty.

For those of you who'd like to see beauty in each moment of your life...

## Do This:

Relax your body and take a few calming breaths. Allow your whole body to relax. If you'd like to tighten and open your fists two times to remind your body of that wonderful relief of tension, do that now.

When you're ready, think this: "I automatically set an aspect of my focus on the beauty that is in each moment of my life."

Now, let go of that thought, which will give it maximum opportunity to develop without any interference.

You have now set your intention to experience beauty in each moment. This is your new default setting.

With the new understanding of yourself and your life as a work of art and the beauty inherent in each moment, let's appreciate even more of you.

## Viewing the scenes of my life from varying angles.

Read the following words, and sit with them for a moment:

> ***"I wonder about seeing the scenes of my life in new ways, and the benefits I will feel as a result."***

The thoughts that follow are designed to support you in expanding your ways of experiencing life, situations, people, yourself, and your understanding of it all. This will ultimately inspire you to let go of the tightness and tension caused by narrow, confined thinking. Be on the lookout for other insights that can pop up: you notice that your life is really interesting, for example, or that upsets can be decoded to reveal treasures, or that words have sound vibrations that land upon you in various ways, or that you are choosing words that more exactly represent what you mean to communicate. Keep a record of these. You will be amazed at what there is to appreciate that you did not see before.

As you consider what I'm saying, you are allowing the energy of these words to soften and actually heal whatever is within you that needs this kind of attention. In these days of cosmic support for emotional growth, it seems unnecessary to dig up all the relics of life that are hardening, limiting, destructive, and obsolete thoughts and beliefs that have been wrecking havoc in your mind and life for years. If you feel called to explore some specifics from the past, then there is benefit in your doing so; however, it is not necessary to unearth it all.

Consider this angle:

**_The way I experience myself, situations, other
people, thoughts, and feelings is seen through
the eyes of my lifetime of understandings,
and is colored by my original conclusions and
decisions made when I was a child._**

Those conclusions and decisions were made through childhood naivety and immaturity. This child-produced thinking has been repeating over and over in your conscious and subconscious mind for decades. It has become habituated, and it's running amok on automatic as the background of your adult life. As you seek to problem solve and discover better ways of living, these outmoded conclusions and decisions take you down self-sabotaging paths of untruths.

As children, we look to connect the dots of things in order to make some sense out of what we see, sense, and feel. The truth is that these dots have little to do with each other, and our connecting them has led us to erroneous conclusions and totally irrelevant and counter-productive decisions.

An example is that many of us grew up associating anger with violence as we witnessed them both at the same time. We understandably connected them and went on automatically assuming that they always go together. This is a common yet erroneous conclusion we made in childhood. Believing that anger and violence always go together prevents people from recognizing anger as a separate and acceptable human emotion. Believing that anger and violence go together also induces fear, which can inhibit even thinking about anger. And this can be the basis of suppression and stuffed feelings. Stuffed, denied, and avoided feelings are a huge component of depression, which is prevalent in our society.

Here's the adult angle on that:

### *"It is possible for me to feel safe experiencing anger and expressing anger in respectful ways."*

No need to think about this. Just sit with the energy of this idea.

*(However, if you are a survivor of childhood physical sexual/emotional abuse, it is important to absorb the concept that you are free to bring the feeling of safety into this moment. You are the sole author of your experience and it falls to you to choose safety at this*

*time. If you are in an abusive situation at this time, it is wise to remove yourself from the situation and get help to do so if need be.)*

Now that you have allowed this idea to sit upon and take root in the fertile ground of your mind, new and associated thoughts will emerge. I wonder what they will be. Watch for them. Allow them to come to you.

Just the awareness that the lines between the dots can be erased brings fresh air and lots of space into the jumble of erroneous connections that you made as a child.

And here's great news: There is no need to think up what those misconnections are. It's enough to breathe in that the misconnecting lines are already starting to dissolve. You'll likely notice a new appreciation of aspects of yourself, your life, and of others as a result of this.

Take time now to sit with this thought:

There are strengths, beauty, talents, abilities, nuances, meaning, value, choices, clarity, skills, and newness for you to appreciate about yourself and your life. These form *the wealth of you*.

All the work you've done to date is enabling you to look with finer discernment on all aspects of yourself and your life.

Relax your body and pretend that this thought
is an easy chair. Take a seat and snuggle in.
Dwell for a little while in this thought.

RELAX

When you are ready, go on.

Here's another example of how childhood conclusions and decisions can set up attitudes a person lives by. As you read this next thought, allow it to wash over you. You can invite your consciousness to expand in many healing ways.

When you were a little baby in a crib, you were undoubtedly crying at some point because you were hungry. Your mom, who was a very loving person, had stomach problems and was stuck in the bathroom. She was feeling so sick that she didn't hear you. Some time passes and you think, "She's not coming." Maybe you cry louder and harder and get very worked up. As you become physically exhausted, you think, "Nobody's coming; no one hears me." As little children, we make it all about us, and so you concluded, "I'm invisible, I have no value, I'm worthless" (or something similar). Based on this conclusion, comes a decision about how you are going to conduct yourself going forward. You decide any of the following, or something else that's still along these lines:

"I'm going to cry louder and louder until I get someone's attention."

"What's the use? No one's going to hear me. I'll just be quiet. In fact, I'll never express a need ever again—not to anyone."

"I'll go out of my way to do everything right and perfectly so that I get noticed, and for sure my needs will get met then."

"I'm going to take care of everyone else, and I will never let anyone take care of me."

You can see how these made-in-childhood conclusions and decisions form the basis for attitudes and behaviors in adult life. This is how they set the style of your relating to yourself and to others.

Your attitudes and approaches to problem solving and to life were developed by you as a child who was rightly seeking to make the best of things and feel safe. And whatever those behavioral decisions were, they were great at the time because they protected you, ensuring you would make it through to adulthood. And they worked because, here you are.

Children are lightweights in life, as they are seen as having no personal authority. You were vulnerable to that attitude from adults and the effects of all that was going on around. You (as are all children) were extremely sensitive and impressionable to the direct impact of the words and actions of the adults who were physically so much larger than you. And if you had parents or caretakers who threw their weight around in a bullying manner, you took the effect of that as well. You were also impacted by the uncontrolled behavior and blurted words of other children.

You have been jarred in many ways during childhood. Perhaps your whole body clenched up when your first-grade teacher reprimanded the child next to you. Maybe your parents yelled at your brother a lot and you witnessed it without being the target. Maybe you took direct hits physically or verbally from others. The point is that you've innocently—with no self-blame—made many, many destructive conclusions about yourself and created what were ultimately self-sabotaging decisions as a result. You have carried these on into adulthood.

It has been said that our aware conscious living is from only 7 percent of our total consciousness. The other 93 percent of all we know and all that we've lived

through—which includes early conclusions and decisions—are in and operating from our subconscious.
This means that your automatic attitudes and knee-jerk
reactions (and for our purpose here I'm referring to those
attitudes that limit the full expression of your creative
energy) are acting out, uncontrolled, from under your
surface (from your subconscious) and, until now, have
been out of your reach. So this explains how, no matter
how much you want to stop eating sugar, you may not
be successful while you are working at cross currents with
perhaps a decision in your subconscious from childhood
that says, "if they don't take care of me, I'll do it myself."
That little person inside you may be taking care of herself
by eating candy, i.e., sugar. She's just a little girl, after all.


Let's relax again into calm
before we move on.

# Healing for the little one.

Take a moment now to call calm into the room and to breathe it in through your nose, taking it into your lungs and witnessing the calm flowing into your bloodstream, and then easily and gently flowing out into the cells nourishing every part of you.

Feel the calm within you and feel surrounded by the calm in the air around you.

Allow the little child in you to relax and B R E A T H E in and absorb the calm.

She's waited a very long time for this. All the bad experiences in her life are really past. Let her glance behind her and let her know that all those upsets of childhood are really way back there in her childhood. They're in another time and another place; that was then and this is now.

She's here now with you and she's safe, because even when you don't know how to handle something as an adult, you will get help for you both. She really is safe now because there really is a grown-up who is taking care of her.

Let her know that her only responsibility is creativity and playfulness, and that you will take care of all the adult responsibilities.

Take a deep relaxing breath and settle into the newness of your relationship with your little girl.

Continue to allow healing as you keep reading.

Take a moment now and notice the warm, healing feeling in the center of your chest. Your heart center.

Notice the yellow glow of that warmth and feel it getting stronger and stronger.

BREATHE

Now send that warm, healing glow from your heart center to the heart center of the little girl, and notice her taking that in.

Notice the look on her face as she takes in these healing, soothing, resolving energies, allowing her to relax and let go.

If she needs additional reassurance, give it to her.

You yourself are healing and you are the healing parent for her and are in her heart; she knows this.

It's time to give her what she's always needed to hear. Tell her all the things she's needed to hear and was never told.

Take plenty of time to do this.

When this feels complete to you, take her into your heart and let her know that this is her new home where she is free to love and be loved.

Relax with her into this feeling. Take as long as you both need.

This is a good place to take a break from reading and go about some of your daily activities. Be aware of subtle and even major changes in the way things look to you. No need to search for these changes, just allow them to come into your awareness.

Now that you've reached this point, if you feel the need to write down your thoughts and feelings as an adult or as the little girl in you, now would be a good time.

*You are doing great.*

You're seeing a great deal more to appreciate about yourself and things and people you're involved with.

Here's another angle through which to appreciate yourself and your life:

**"Today I can choose my attitude about my experience. I choose my attitude."**

Now that attitudes developed in childhood have been understood, you can read what follows, knowing that this understanding serves your self-appreciation, you, and your life as the most beautiful work of art ever!

"But I feel awful," you say. So why would you choose this awfulness?

Take a moment now and let your body relax.

Call the energy of calm into the room.

Start to breathe the energy of calm in through your nose, into your lungs.

Allow that energy to move out into your blood, nourishing all the cells, molecules, and atoms of your body and full self.

Remember, your feelings are definitely to be appreciated.

All your feelings, even feeling awful.

You can, with your imagination or by setting the thought intention, soften the edges around your feelings, especially around the ones you haven't liked. It is not required that you like or dislike people, traits, or situations.

**Actually, a liking vs. disliking approach is one of the most limiting approaches.**

If you looked at a painting or other work of art through only like or dislike, and dismissed that which you disliked, that action would gravely limit what you could get out of the experience. Some people are aware that they are interested in "getting the most out of life" or "having the fullest experience of life." Liking and disliking draws your attention away from all the zoom-in details and all the zoom-out overview that's available in each experience. You've heard of people who see things in black or white, well, liking and disliking falls into the black-and-white category.

As you allow liking and disliking to move over to the side,

making room for more self-appreciation, you can take in this idea: As birds are meant to fly and fish are meant to swim, humans are meant to feel, and that means the full range of all feelings.

It's a good opportunity now to breathe and take a relieving sigh.

ahhhh

**"All feelings are natural, and I'm supposed to have them."**

Let's look at how liking and disliking occurred in your life. We'll also see how the negative effects of liking and disliking are being undone with your new knowledge.

When you were little, you got the idea that some feelings or expressions of feelings were not okay, and so they were squashed—suppressed, inhibited, feared, pressed down, kept from, avoided. It's possible that childhood feelings went underground because they were too much for you to deal with.

As an adult, you continue to spend a great deal of time and energy to keep these feelings down in the subconscious in favor of dealing with everyday life. But these suppressed feelings can't stay inside forever. As these suppressed feelings push their way out, you overreact to situations. Like when you've felt your crying is way more than seems fitting, or you burst out in anger more than is appropriate for particular situations. Other people's assessments of your behavior are irrelevant here since those people are not inside of you, knowing what measures of feelings have or have not been adequately expressed in your life. Only your inner sense gives the accurate information about you. This burst of emotion is due to triggered, pent-up feelings from unexpressed episodes of the past, which reside in your subconscious.

Feeling overwhelmed? Let's reframe that thought.

Instead, how about thinking, "Look how much there is to appreciate!"

In case you are wondering how to deal with being triggered, we will deal with that topic in the chapter titled "Honoring Myself."

With feelings emerging, as if out of nowhere, and thoughts coming into your thinking, as if out of your control, choosing your attitude or approach could be a real mystery.

There is a philosophy that says that all pain, confusion, and fatigue results from pressing feelings down and away (avoiding, keeping from, denying,) from expression.

Reversing this is very doable.

You've experienced this already in your reading here. Tightening your fists was the same energy as pressing the feelings down and away. The opening of your palms transformed that tightening and tensing. It actually changed the tightening, tensing energy into the energy of allowing and openness. You felt the change take place.

Sit in this experience for a few minutes and allow it to anchor into your being.

Take a few relaxing breaths.

Let the muscles in your body relax and let go.

Let go, and open to receive.

Call calming energy into the room and allow it to waft all around you.

Tighten your fists and then open your palms to receive calming, clearing energy.

As you take it in through your breathing, also take it in through your skin.

Let it wash lightly through you.

As you continue to relax and bathe in the calm, feel yourself open to allow the next ideas to wash over and through you.

**Decisions based on benefit to you.**

There's another angle through which to appreciate yourself and those around you. Take a look at this statement:

> *All the decisions you've made were made based on a bottom-line benefit for you. Even the decisions you haven't liked.*

The truth is—and no one can really dispute this—you are the main star and no one can upstage you. They can try and probably have. Others in your life can only be candidates for the Best Supporting Actor Award. Only you can receive the Best Actor Award.

And here's another undeniable truth:

**You are the sole authority in your life, which means you are the only one who chooses your attitude toward your experiences.**

Others can have their opinions but those opinions, in truth, are theirs alone. Unless you *want* to adopt their ideas as yours, they have nothing to do with you. If their idea can enhance your view of yourself in a productive way, then you might want to think twice about how adopting that idea could be useful.

Here's more good news!

Thoughts that you've adopted from others that are untrue, no longer serve you, and are obsolete, can be UN-adopted.

## Use this now.

First, relax your body.

Call calm into the room.

Breathe in the calm, and then set the intention to un-adopt thoughts you have adopted from others that are untrue, that no longer serve you, and that are obsolete.

You may have misgivings about some decisions you've made or actions you've taken in your life. You may feel, "If I had only chosen that *other* way," or "My whole life would be different had I only done…" or "I knew I should have…" or "How could I have thought…?" Misgivings, guilt, self-criticism, putting yourself down, and wishing otherwise are often accompanied by anxiety and distress.

The way to *dissolve* the adverse effects of this negativity is to consider this very neutralizing idea:

> **"All decisions I've made, I made based on a benefit for my growth. Even the decisions I haven't liked."**

You can probably identify several decisions that you haven't liked but that you learned great lessons from. Even behaviors that you've chosen that seemed counter-productive are likely to have been helpfully defensive. You were defending your safety or trying to stay safe from a real danger or from a triggered feeling of fear. It is time to realize that not only is there is no blame, but blaming yourself or others is self-sabotaging. Let the blaming go! Set the intention to let any remaining blame leave with your every exhale.

What's left after the blame is gone is your natural inner problem-solving ability—your intuition and inner self.

OKAY, TAKE A FULL BREATH.

# BREATHE

Take a moment to explore the new options and feelings that you suddenly have room for because that old blame is now gone. Without the blame, it is easier to picture yourself as the work of art that you truly are.

Now that you have room for new thoughts and feelings, allow the idea that there are benefits—at times hidden— for all your inclinations and actions. Invite the benefits into your awareness so that you can make conscious choices based on great additional information. Once the benefits are brought to light, they are no longer empowering behavior and choices propelled by old conclusions and decisions. You can now say, "I'll keep this one and let that one go." The choices will be yours.

CHAPTER THREE

# Step 3:
# Healing My Inner Wisdom

## No Need to Look Elsewhere

So now, relax into your openness.

Take several slow and relaxing breaths.

With each breath, allow any tension and tightness to drift
away from your body.

As you do this, your body naturally becomes relaxed.

Enjoy this relaxation. Allow your mind to go to your favorite, most relaxing place and to settle in there.

Allow your thoughts to float by above you, like clouds on a beautifully clear day.

Allow your emotions to relax and soften as you take a few more relaxing breaths.

This is a welcome rest from your day's activities.

If you feel like sighing in relief, go ahead and do that.

As you are relaxing, bring to mind a trait, talent, or characteristic that you wish you had. Don't think about it. Just allow one to come to mind. If there is more than one, notice which one has the most energy at this time. For example, you may be picturing yourself with more courage or more playfulness.

Now, call the energy of that trait, talent, or characteristic into the room and gently breathe it in. Feel it come into your nasal passages and down into your lungs. Breathe in this trait several times before going on.

Imagine it flowing out of your lungs and into your blood-stream. Feel relaxation and the energy pass through your blood and into the cells of your nervous system, relaxing, releasing, and letting go.

Then into the cells of your muscles, relaxing, releasing, and letting go.

Then into the cells of your bones, relaxing, releasing, and letting go.

Then into the cells of your lymphatic system, relaxing, releasing, and letting go.

And into the cells of all your organs and other systems, relaxing, releasing, and letting go.

Allow this energy to saturate your entire self—the molecules, the atoms, and down to the subatomic particles.

**There is healing that occurs each time you relax. And the more you relax your body, the clearer and more alert is your mind.**

Your *Inner Wisdom* brought this ability to your alert mind.

Rest in this clarity for a few minutes.

When you are ready, let's go on.

## The treasure within myself: hearing my Inner Wisdom and acknowledging it.

Among the many treasures within yourself that are available for you to appreciate is your Innate Inner Wisdom.

At first it may not seem readily accessible. But to see, sense, or feel it, you only need to intend to do so. We only see what we focus on, and your focus can go from one thing to another, as if on automatic. You may not know that you can direct and concentrate your focus any time you choose to. Choosing to focus is no different than shining a light on something in order to see it.

The following is an empowered declaration expressing your intention to detect, see, sense, feel, become aware of, and know your Innate Inner Wisdom.

Say out loud (or emphatically within yourself) three times:

### *"I concentrate my focus on detecting my Innate Inner Wisdom."*

### *"I concentrate my focus on detecting my Innate Inner Wisdom."*

### *"I concentrate my focus on detecting my Innate Inner Wisdom."*

There is transformative power in emphatically declaring an intention. (That's a thought worth remembering and even contemplating its usefulness in other areas of your life as well.)

**Your Inner Wisdom is indirectly visible (i.e., communicating with you), no matter what.**

Have you ever second guessed yourself and later on realized you would have been better off had you made your original choice? That you actually had a sense about the rightness of that choice early on but still discounted it?

That first choice you made—the wiser choice—was your Inner Wisdom showing itself.

Remember the times you have deliberated over purchasing a sweater or a dress or shoes, or you deliberated over which is the best value for the money regarding a furniture purchase. "Should I buy this one, or that one?" Maybe you even labored over the decision before ultimately making it.

Your smartest self made the decision, based on the wisest choice at that moment. Even if afterward you judged the purchase to be frivolous, the decision was based on enjoyment, or the perception of need, or some other really good benefit, and so it was your Inner Wisdom that chose for you.

When you think about it this way, you can see how your Inner Wisdom has been communicating with you all along.

Another way it communicates is when you get a hunch about something. If the hunch is accurate, this is another way your Inner Wisdom shows up. If your hunch is inaccurate, it was still your Inner Wisdom that instigated your thinking.

How about the times you have become very certain about something that you were previously uncertain about? Or when you hear something someone else says, and you feel deeply that what that person says is truly the way it is, or you feel deeply that it is not so? Another time your Inner Wisdom communicates with you is when you get a deep sense that something you read or heard resonates with you. These are all examples of your Inner Wisdom's presence and its activity within you, confirming and validating your choices and moving you along in your growth.

Another way your Inner Wisdom communicates with you is when you get an uh-oh feeling. Something feels a little off, or a lot off. It could be a sense that you shouldn't make a particular choice or speak aloud a particular thought or feeling. At some point, you may have actually disregarded or overridden that sense. It might have been that the uh-oh feeling was very faint, and you didn't recognize that it was there until after the fact. It may have been that you were getting a clear message to make a different choice, yet you kept saying to yourself, "Nah," and insisting you continue along the lines you were originally choosing. Later you may have felt upset, irritated, and distressed over the decision you made. You felt out of sync with yourself.

Knowing now that this was your Inner Wisdom communicating with you, you can have a new curiosity about it. Since you have set your intention to experience your Innate Inner Wisdom, you will be noticing it more and more.

Your Innate Inner Wisdom was in its purest state when you were little. Much life and living has happened since then, covering over some of the depth and richness of your Inner Wisdom. Sometimes seeking your Inner Wisdom can be like opening a gift, unpacking a gift package, or opening a treasure chest.

## Decoding your relationship with your Inner Wisdom.

It's true that the voice, sense, or feeling of your Inner Wisdom can also be down deeper, beneath many experiences in your life. It can even be drowned out by a strong sense of right and wrong, which you developed in childhood, adopted from adults in your childhood, or developed over the years. Some of your early caretakers' values have become ingrained in you. It's possible that rebellion against those values is also engrained in you. If some of the strong senses you adopted during childhood belonged to the adults that you adopted them from, then those senses have become your default setting and might not even be yours.

But your own natural Inner Wisdom that you had as a child is still within you.

Fully or clearly hearing your Inner Wisdom may also be blocked by the sense of things you adopted from your peers. We're all familiar with the idea of how important peer connections are during the impressionable and formative years of early childhood and adolescence. Subconscious conclusions overshadowing Inner Wisdom can be:

*I'm not smart*

*I'm the smartest*

*I'm too smart*

*I'm ugly*

*I'm pretty*

*I'm not good at math*

*I can't remember details for tests*

*I can't do art*

*The boys like me*

*There's something wrong with me*

Hearing your Inner Wisdom can also be blocked by the sense of things you adopted from those you've looked up to, whose opinions became more valuable than your own through their declaration of importance or your decision that they knew better than you. The prevailing general opinion of society may also have been selected by you as wiser than your own Inner Wisdom's opinion as well.

Not hearing your Innate Inner Wisdom might be behind any negative self-judgment you have or an idea that you picked up long ago, which questions your ability to think things through or make decisions or certain types of decisions. You may feel confident making decisions concerning schooling for your kids and scheduling, but not concerning family investments, or whether or not to start your own business.

A general feeling of being not good enough can keep your Inner Wisdom out of your awareness as well.

But no worries.

Your increasing awareness is already inviting your Inner Wisdom to come to the surface to reveal itself. You are in the process of unwrapping your relationship with your own Inner Wisdom in order to recognize it fully and access it readily.

Since we only see or hear what we focus on, it's very productive that you are taking the time now to direct your focus and be open to experiencing your Inner Wisdom.

Recognizing that your Inner Wisdom is communicating with you and focusing your attention in its direction allows you to see, sense, feel, and experience it.

**Your Inner Wisdom is present in every moment of your life.**

Take a moment and sit with this thought.

Read it over a few times.

Allow the meaning of these words to seep deeply into you.

Consider the benefits of becoming able to access this treasure within you.

Take as much time as you need to allow the benefits to become anchored within you. List them if you like.

When you are ready, let's move on.

While you read the next section, I invite you to gain additional appreciation of the hidden story of the artwork that is your life.

## How my Inner Wisdom slipped out of view.

There is often so much going on every day and life is so fast-paced that you can whiz right by your Inner Wisdom and not see or sense it in the blur.

As a child, you were naturally aligned with Inner Wisdom. You may or may not remember this. At the time, it was your natural state. You were your pure Inner Wisdom in action. Unfortunately, most, if not everyone, has been distracted away from their Inner Wisdom by early life experiences.

Allow the words of the examples in the following paragraphs to wash over you. Allow any limiting thoughts and beliefs that no longer serve you to come to the surface and float away.

It's been a parenting style forever for parents to direct (sometimes with an authoritarian flair) the focus of their children on what they, as adults, want, and what they want for the child's best development. If you candidly expressed your Inner Wisdom when you were younger and even through your teen years, and if the adults didn't agree with you, it's likely that they tried to talk you out of it. Some parents feel that because children are young and therefore lacking in life's experience, the child's opinion could not possibly be credible, even when that opinion is about the child himself. An even more extreme invalidation of a child's opinion is the old expression, "Children are to be seen and not heard." The message to the child was that "your opinion is nothing compared to my grown-up opinion."

Another style some parents have is to be very permissive. They over-indulged their children and made them the entire focus of attention. But when a child doesn't get healthy discipline and gets caught up in commanding the family's attention, the child is then distracted away from his or her own Inner Wisdom.

Even the most well-intentioned and educated parents who try not to take away their child's sense of self, and who validate their child and do their best to speak the truth within a context of unconditional love, can also inadvertently and unknowingly position a child to disregard his or her Inner Wisdom voice.

Through the socialization process of attending school, a child's Inner Wisdom has to be routinely disregarded in favor of conforming to group rules for behavior. Going to school each day (like it or not), doing what you were told, focusing with the whole class, and doing required tasks are examples of this.

Through repetition of this squelching, you and everyone else were conditioned *out* of focusing on your Inner Wisdom. You were conditioned to focus outside yourself for wisdom. You may have even decided that your inner sense wasn't worth much or was even worthless. You're not alone; many people feel this way as adults.

As a result, not only did you stop being your spontaneous, natural self through your Innate Inner Wisdom, you also lost touch with the fact that it was there at all. It's gotten buried beneath have-tos, obligations, societal norms, pleasing people, avoiding doing the frowned-upon things, trying to do the "right" things, not taking care of yourself, and being unconsciously swept up in the activities of life.

You may have also have had grief and loss when you were little, causing shock and shutting you down emotionally. Shutting down, even as a protection, shuts you off from your own Inner Wisdom. For example, a parent or other person close to you may have died or left you. You may have been emotionally abandoned, i.e., the surviving parent is not emotionally present to meet your needs. Being molested or emotionally abused are also reasons to shut down emotionally.

As a child, your internal defending against the loss, loneliness, and devastation of divorce and illness and economic devastation can overshadow and completely bury your Innate Inner Wisdom, until you are ready to heal.

**The shutting down lasts until it is opened up.**

Here's some good news:

This is all behind you now; it's in the past. That was then; this is now. Imagine looking behind you. See the pain way back there, far away from you as you sit here in the present.

Take a moment now.

B R E A T H E in relaxation and openness.

B R E A T H E relaxation deep into your lungs.

Know that with each breath, the relaxation goes out through your lungs and into your bloodstream, relaxing all your organs and body systems, all your cells, and their molecules, atoms, and subatomic particles.

Breathe relaxation throughout your body, mind, and energy field. While looking back behind you, where the past has been, notice that all the thoughts, feelings, beliefs, events, and people who have stood between you and your ability to hear your own Innate Inner Wisdom have shrunken up so tiny that they are now so far away in the past you can barely see them from your vantage point here in the present.

If you have a sigh of relief, B R E A T H E it out now.

As you have been reading this and allowing all the words of the examples to wash through you, you have been cleansing away the negative effects that have clouded your Innate Inner Wisdom. The clearing effect has taken place and you are now free to consciously access your resource. Your Innate Inner Wisdom.

The healing awareness that you now have has opened the lid of the treasure chest of your Innate Inner Wisdom, allowing it to come out to the light of day, allowing it to breathe the fresh air.

ahhhh

## Slow down to receive the messages.

Slowing the speed of your experiences enables you to see, sense, feel, hear, and recognize your own Inner Wisdom's messages for you and its responses to your inquiries, questions, and requests for guidance. Life can be made much richer and more interesting when you slow down your experience. It can also lead the way to eliminating exhaustion, tiredness, and energy drain. As we discussed in chapter two, you can do this by turning down the speed-control dial. When you slow your experience down, you can relax into seeing and appreciating much more of what's occurring and can see choices and opportunities clearly.

*Your Inner Wisdom has been underneath the surface, waiting for you to call it up.*

And it also has a recommendation for you about anything that interests you.

## Calling up your Inner Wisdom—with ease.

Accessing this treasure, this resource within you, is started simply by setting the intention with your mind to access your Inner Wisdom. You have done this once at the beginning of this chapter's process, so you know how to do it and have the tool available anytime you want to use it.

Repeatedly seeking access to your Inner Wisdom forges a groove that provides ready access as a default setting.

Let's continue the process.

Take a few relaxing breaths, and call the energy of calm into the room.

B R E A T H E in that calm.

BREATHE

Take as much time as you need to breathe it all the way in, throughout all aspects of your being. Through the lungs, into the bloodstream, and out into the organs, nervous system, muscles, bones, lymphatic system, brain, cells, molecules, atoms, subatomic particles, and the energy field around your body, as you've done before.

When you are calm and relaxed, say out loud or strongly within yourself:

"I call you forth, my Inner Wisdom. Come into my consciousness so that I may see, sense, feel, and hear you."

Sit quietly and allow the meaning of this to seep deeply into you.

Allow as much time as you need for this sitting.

## Calling in my Inner Wisdom each morning.

A great time to invite forward your Inner Wisdom is just before you get out of bed in the morning. Calling forth your Inner Wisdom first thing in the morning sets it as a specific focus for your entire day. Concentrate for a moment each morning on the following:

## THE MORNING CALL

*"I set the intention to access the treasure of my Inner Wisdom today."*

As the day goes on, you will notice your Inner Wisdom reveal itself more and more. At the end of the day, when you head for bed, review the day. You will see all the times your Inner Wisdom appeared.

If you have trouble remembering to do this, I have included in the back of the book the text for "Call My Inner Wisdom," which you can copy and keep by your bedside. The note will remind you to invite your Inner Wisdom as a part of each morning.

This will take *practically no time* to do every day, and it will become integrated into your thought process so it is as automatic as breathing.

CHAPTER FOUR

# Step 4:
# Honoring My Self

## Following My Inner Inclinations

Continuing to allow yourself to see, sense, feel, or hear
the voice of your Innate Inner Wisdom actually creates a
pathway in your brain/being/energy field/experience so it
can become a default setting. After a while, you will notice
that it becomes easier to see, sense, feel, or hear the
voice of your Inner Wisdom. Don't be surprised when
you start to get spontaneous *yes* and *no* messages from
within. This can even be about things like which top to
wear, which shoes to purchase, what food is your best

choice. The yes-or-no sense can be bold or very subtle, like an inkling, a hunch, a fleeting thought. You might even hear in your mind—or sense or feel—a direction, such as "brush your teeth."

Throughout your reading of this book, you have become more and more relaxed with the presence of your own Inner Wisdom, which has now become your Inner Wise Self, the voice of your Inner Wisdom.

We talked about slowing down in order to have more opportunity to experience nuances of feelings, desires, inspiration, and awarenesses. In doing this, you are allowing yourself to see, appreciate, and value the work of art that is you and your life—your daily life, each of your days. Each day is its own work of art. You can even zero in closer: each episode during the day is its own work of art. Each encounter with a person. Each hour. Each fifteen-minute period, and so on.

This slowing down, recognizing, and *appreciating approach* to the movie of your life puts you in a good position to detect subtle inclinations of your heart. These subtle inclinations are another way to experience the encouragement of your Inner Wise Self.

Now, each leaning of your heart is a whisper from your Inner Wise Self. "What's over here?" "What's over there?" "Do you want to...?" "What about...?"

It can be a great comfort to know that you have a source of wisdom tailored specifically for you and that's right inside of you. While others may have their opinions about what is best for you, and you might even choose to consider their opinions, it's a wonderful thing to know that you have your own Inner Wise Self as your consultant. This consultant is available 24/7.

## Allow yourself to flow forward.

Following the inclination and direction of your Wise Self is a way to follow your natural path of development, to allow yourself to flow forward.

This is a good place to stop for a minute and take in the full meaning of these words:

**Allow yourself to flow forward.**

Using your mind, first (simply by deciding to do so), invite the feeling of **openness** into the room.

Breathe it in and send it all through your body and emotional self as well.

Use your mind, your imagination, and pretend.

Relax for a moment into your openness.

**Allow yourself to flow forward.**

Now look at the word "**Allow**."

The energy of the word includes a type of giving permission for entry or continuation.

It could be like moving one step to the side and gesturing with your arm out forward and to the side, giving a show of support and gentle direction for the something to flow forward. This gesture signifies a true honoring of your movement forward. We're talking here about you giving your self, your energy (your *natural* energy), permission to flow forward in your life.

Permission to move forward doesn't come from anyone else. It's yours to give and yours to receive.

Allow the following words to resonate in your mind:

**Following the inclination and direction of my Inner Wise Self**

**is the same as**

**Following my natural path of development. Allowing myself to flow forward.**

Stop reading here
and sit with this
thought for a while.

## ᔬ LET'S GO ON

What should you do during those times when you notice that you are not following your inner guidance? Let's talk about that.

In your life, you may experience internal resistance to moving forward or undertaking specific tasks on the way to accomplishing your goals. You may experience fear and notice that, in response, you shy away or turn away from your goal, which sends you in the opposite direction of what your innate, honest gut says is the fitting direction for you at the moment. You're turning away from the direction your Wise Self invited you to follow.

Remember, it's already a great accomplishment to hear the direction of your Inner Wise Self. Following it is the next natural step.

You may notice that you are following your inner guidance more and more. In some instances, just allowing new information to wash through you facilitates easily choosing to follow your inner guidance. Perhaps you are already recognizing the places where you do this naturally, without any effort.

You may also notice that there are times when you override your inner guidance and make a different choice. You may discover that you hear, sense, or feel a clear direction and, as mentioned above, you still turn away and do the opposite. Or you seem to be drawn to every distraction imaginable, which interferes with following the guidance of your Inner Wise Self.

Remember:

**To know you is to love you!**

Allowing yourself to be curious at this point will serve you well. Sometimes when you don't follow your inner voice, you are being called to discover a different path and to appreciate something else about the beautiful work of art that is you.

Allowing yourself to become curious entails a sincere desire to "find out"—even if you're cautious or have trepidation.

In the true spirit of "finding out," I've included several questions in this chapter as a gift to you. Their purpose is to gather new information that will contribute to clearing out that energy of reluctance.

It's important that you proceed through these questions without negative self-judgment. This means no negative self-judgment out front or in the wings. If you need help with that, here's a way to clear out any negative self-judgment. Up to this point, we have discussed your Inner Wise Self as a consultant when, in fact, it is also an active helper. Ask your Inner Wise Self, your spiritual connection, or your higher consciousness to lift any negative self-judgment from you, so you will get new information that is not tainted or colored by any preconceived negative notions. As your helpers lift any energy of judgment, try to experience or imagine yourself pushing those judgment thoughts up and out. Imagine the energy of judgment and preconceived notions leaving the cellular structure of your body, including the molecules, atoms, and subatomic particles of your entire being.

Now, without the energy of judgment in your being, you'll be able to ask for, recognize, and receive answers to the upcoming questions. Remember, we're asking these questions solely to gather information, not to devise any action. Follow the answers as deeply as they may go. They may go down winding paths and give you more questions and eventually more answers. Don't worry if you can't remember all the ways the information progresses. Set your intention to sit in the energies and the feelings that come up. Appreciate sensing the feelings as they flow through you and out of you.

Bring up the sincere spirit of "I want to find out…" as we prepare to start the questions. Now, call to mind the most recent time you heard guidance from your Inner Wise Self and didn't follow it, even though you knew the guidance was the best guidance for you. Have this situation in mind as you ask yourself each one of the questions in the following process.

# Spend a Moment:

Get in touch with the "turn away,"
or energy of reluctance.

***"Who or what am I really turning
away from?"***

No thinking! Just allow a person or
place to come to you. Make a mental
note or actually jot down what comes to
you. Now, go on to the next question.

***"How am I using the energy of
turning away to hurt, harm, abuse,
or sabotage myself?"***

Be specific. The next question will help
you with this.

**"When I turn away from my guidance, what am I robbing myself of?"**

Relax and contemplate this question. Allow some things to come to mind, and jot them down. Spend as much time as you need on this one. Get as full of an appreciation as you can of the impact from your turning away from the guidance of your own Inner Wise Voice.

Here are a few examples: "I'm robbing myself of my destiny, my fulfillment and satisfaction in life, my development, and whatever I would discover during my natural development, such as relationships, intimacy, time with loved ones, relationships free of my projections on to them, achievements, or discovery of new talents." The list is endless.

*"What is the real beneficial gain I get when I turn away from my inner voice?"*

You might say, "Beneficial gain? Why would I want that?" Remember, early on in your life, turning away was a safety maneuver. At least, it was in your mind at that time.

Just like the rest of us, when you were little you had many instances in which your emotional needs were not met. That's just the way it is for most kids, even with the best, most well-intentioned parents. And so, at an early age, you had a response every time your emotional needs were not met. Many of us squelched our emotions and kept our mouths shut, because expressing an idea or experience did not feel safe. As we've discussed, you consequently developed safety strategies, which then hardened into habits. And one of them was to turn away.

Your subconscious, which is the predominant 93 percent that drives your life, steers you away from your Inner Wise Voice. So, guess what? You get an underlying secondary gain from turning away. Even though you act in direct opposition to your inner voice, you receive benefits which you are not aware of. These benefits might be safety, a buffer from having to think, or a soothing comfort for some kind of negative and inaccurate projection, perception, or upsetting thought.

So ask yourself again, with real curiosity and wonder: "What is the benefit—the secondary gain—to turning away?"

Expand your awareness to include the answers to these questions each time you notice yourself subtly shy away or boldly turn away from your Inner Wise Voice. Contemplate your answers, and really own that this is what you do and what you think and experience. Doing so allows the blockage and the reluctance energy to dissolve and be healed.

Through owning the answers to the above questions, you allow yourself to become aware of layers of reluctance, resistance, and outmoded self-constructed protections.

**The more layers of reluctance and resistance that you allow yourself to become aware of, the easier it is to follow your Inner Wise Voice.**

Once you get into a routine of questioning and decoding the benefits of turning away, your understanding will reach a point of critical mass. You will have gotten out of your own way. Your energy will then completely shift, and you will become interested in discovering where your Innate Inner Wise Voice will lead you. You become eager to fan the flame of your creativity while following your Inner Wise Voice.

The more you notice and attend to turning away the energy in this way, the more often you will be following your inner guidance. This approach frees you up. And once you are freed up, following the inner guidance is natural, and you flow with it.

## Honor Yourself.

This is another way of looking at it: honoring yourself.

I think you could be saying to yourself right now, "that's a bit much." While you probably agree that you are worth honoring, you may be concerned that there's something a little over the top about this idea. Something like conceit, or a king or a queen honoring themselves. You have done work to bring yourself from feeling diminished to feeling good enough, so you might be wondering, "How far am I to go with this?"

The truth is that many of us have felt "less than" during

our lives and have needed to elevate ourselves all the way up in order to be equal to someone else in our own minds. That has been important and necessary to do. But now, this curiosity to see where your inner voice will lead you is one way of honoring yourself.

Honoring yourself has nothing to do with being egotistical or overblown, rest assured. So what does it mean, exactly, to honor yourself? It means that you are willing to see yourself and your life as worthwhile. The idea that "I am of value" brings this to light within you. It also clears out any traces of limiting thoughts which tell you otherwise.

**Holding yourself in true, positive regard is one of the best things you can do for yourself.**

Freeing yourself to follow the guidance of your own Inner Wise Self is truly *Honoring Your Self*.

When you honor the guidance of your inner self, it's a great feeling. Honoring is really following your inner self's voice, isn't it? For some people, this means selecting the foods at each meal that are best suited to their needs. Even the portion sizes can be guided in this way.

When you follow your Inner Wise Voice, in terms of setting priorities, selecting activities, choosing which actions to take, or what to focus on in each moment, ask yourself these questions:

"Which one is in my highest and best good?"

"Which one is in the highest and best good of all?"

In closing, remember that your Inner Wise Self—which is totally and only attuned to you, your needs, and your best interests—is also available to become your confidante, personal consultant, personal growth partner, and best friend. You can rely on it for anything. How great is that!

Take a breath and allow yourself to process what you've just read.

ahhhh

Don't be surprised if this is a chapter you want to reread several times. And that's a good idea before going on to chapter five.

.

# Step 5:
# Caring for My Self

## The Old Ways and the New Ways

**Allowing Self-Care as a primary background orientation.**

Self-Care is an amazing concept to make your own. It is important to realize that a Self-Care perspective is an essential component to your Inner Freedom. Embracing a Self-Care orientation involves letting go of anything in the way of making caring choices for yourself, such as dissuading attitudes adopted in childhood from caretakers, society, and the people in your life. It also means letting go of having difficulty receiving.

In order to fully appreciate the role of strength and the benefits associated with *owning* **Self-Care** as a primary orientation and activity, it can be helpful to recognize that this is not a fashionable idea in our society.

Take a few relaxing breaths and read the following, but only as background information. Relax as you read it; there will be no test. Allowing the following words to gently and easily wash over you will begin to flush away the limiting thoughts, feelings, and beliefs that have been in your way.

B R E A T H E . Doing this will serve your conditioning for a wonderful experience of continued Self-Care.

**Self-Care vs. selfishness.**

Historically, it has not been fashionable in our society to take care of ourselves, per se. It's not fashionable for women and, I dare say, the term "Self-Care" has never been used by or for men (maybe not even in therapy sessions!).

Self-Care, as mentioned in chapter one, has been

considered selfish. Let's look at the word *selfish*. As a word, selfish means "pertaining to the self," which in and of itself has no negativity associated with it. Like the words *girl* and *girlish*.

Yes, it does pertain to focus on the self. And when considered Self-Care, it needs to be viewed in the healthiest and most growth-producing way, to counteract the negativity that abounds around it.

In our world, unfortunately, self-ish (focus on the self) has gotten a bad rap. It has been associated with exploitation (true, that is a form of self-ishness); is much more than benign, neutral selfishness; and is not what Self-Care is about.

Exploitation is taking unfair advantage of others. All exploitation is selfishness, *but not all self-ishness is exploitation*. Most people assume that when an act is selfish, even in its neutral form (including Self-Care), it is at the expense of others and can actually hurt them.

The problem here is disrespect for boundaries. Self-Care,

however, especially when coupled with kindness, is respectful of you and other people, even if they don't see or feel it that way. When taking Self-Caring actions—like saying "no, thank you" to another's requests or demands, even when done respectfully—you may encounter people who get upset. Perhaps because they're feeling insulted and hurt, they may demand that you stop being Self-Caring and may even call you selfish. When people get used to you saying or acting as if their bad behavior is okay, it's true, they aren't going to like you starting to say "no, thank you" to them.

You allow people to believe their behavior is acceptable when you take care of them emotionally, in a codependent, caretaking way, by doing things for them that they can do for themselves, or by never saying "no, thank you" to their poor behaviors, offerings, gestures, opinions, criticisms, requirements, or demands.

They may feel your new Self-Caring way of being is unfair to them, the same way children whose parents limit their spending on toys or candy say "No fair!" Actually, you *are* eliminating advantages that you had granted them, unwittingly or unconsciously, before you started respecting your own boundaries. So, yes, they might very well feel disadvantaged, and they'll blame you and your Self-Care behavior that, in their eyes, is selfishness. It would be great if they could be supportive of you, but they may not have the emotional maturity to say *yes* to your Self-Care while you are saying *no* to their behavior.

Take a relaxing breath at this point and allow yourself to open. a h h h h .

Set your **intention to allow** this next thought to be very freeing. It's a thought most people don't know about, and it is a great *key to your own health.*

# BREATHE

Breathe and relax and allow.

Ready?

**People who are dissatisfied or even angry with your Self-Caring can feel—and have the right to feel—any way they want, because their feelings are located within them and are under their sole jurisdiction. And, quite frankly, those feelings are none of your business or your concern.**

However, even though it's not your business, it can be okay—as a kindness or courtesy, if you allow it—to *cut them some slack on their new disappointment and loss.* They have lost something valuable that had been extended to them and is now withdrawn. On the other hand, if they treat you badly in response to your new Self-Caring ways, it's best *NOT* to cut them any slack on their bad behavior.

This next concept is very important and may be new to you.

**You can cut them slack on their feelings and not cut them slack on their disrespectful behavior. Accepting their feelings, disappointment, and loss—and not accepting their disrespectful behavior—can both exist simultaneously.**

If this is a new concept for you, stop reading and review it. Sit with it for a while. Contemplate it. After reading this concept, just allow your mind to rest with it for a while.

Allowing this concept to seep deeply into your consciousness will heal many old emotional wounds that kick things up from under the surface where your experiences are stored.

Remember, you are **not** exploiting anyone by taking care of yourself. It's up to them also to take care of themselves when they don't like what's happening or are not getting their way. Certainly, it would feel best to you if they could do this in ways that are respectful to you and to them. The problem is that most other people are not educated about this concept. They know nothing about boundaries and are blinded when their own internal issues are triggered.

(By the way, your behavior triggers other people, even your nice behavior. It's not only nice to be kind to others even when your new Self-Caring behavior is triggering and upsetting them, it's best for your health as well.)

147

Your responsibility is to take care of your self and to do so in as respectful a way as possible. This will support your health and may even be a building block in your relationship with others.

Most people don't think this deeply or carefully about the meaning of words. And so this distinction—the idea of exploitation vs. self-ishness vs. Self-Care—is not talked about much, if at all, in the mainstream of life, i.e., on TV, in the news, or even among most people. So it is likely that, in the common culture, the terms *selfish* and *Self-Care* will continue to be associated with something negative, with the unspoken term *exploitation*.

**The implied association between self attention and exploitation is not true with respect to Self-Care.**

**Let nothing deter you from undertaking the orientation of Self-Care. Your Inner Freedom and health depend upon this.**

**In the health and wellness field, the concept of Self-Care has been gaining ground.**

In the commercial arena, there is a huge Self-Care industry. It focuses primarily on our external selves with loud messages many times a day that suggest how this product or that service are just what we need to give ourselves better this or better that:

*Skin care products*

*Medication for ailments*

*Exercise and medication to lower blood pressure*

*Shiny hair with volume*

*Exercise for body strengthening, weight loss, and counteracting the effects of aging*

*Eat right (whatever that is these days)*

*Botox*

*Plastic surgery*

*Stop smoking*

*Mainstream supermarkets that are starting to carry organic food products*

**Self-Care in a more internal way.**

This idea has been thought of as healthy only since about

2001, when it was more publically introduced by Melody Beattie, who published her book, *Codependent No More*. She brought to public attention numerous ways to leave behind the self-limiting affliction of codependent caretaking.

Even though it might look nice and altruistic on the outside, codependent caretaking is actually a dysfunctional attempt to take care of ourselves through endearing ourselves to others, and seeking appreciation, validation, and even love to compensate for emotional needs that were not met in our childhood. And to make matters worse, this occurs without our awareness. Codependent caretaking of others excludes healthy Self-Care.

Codependence, an immature form of Self-Care we developed in early childhood, was created to protect ourselves from the assault we felt from the power of the adults around us. This is worth contemplating.

We women especially have taken our loving, nurturing, caring selves to a fault, often way too far into serving others *at the exclusion* of even minimally attending to ourselves. In fact, we do others an injustice, rescuing them from necessary learning experiences, which include failure.

When have you emotionally and physically exhausted yourself taking care of others?

Never saying *no* to them directly, or never saying *no* to your own habitual pressure to serve?

They may not even be verbally asking you for anything. In other instances, you may have said *no* in your mind and simply didn't verbalize it. Or you may have said it out loud, only to have been ignored by the other person. You may not have known that it was your next step to validate yourself and set a boundary in a more declarative way, either with speech or with an action. You may not have felt safe enough or have known how to say *no* or *no, thank you* effectively.

When you realize codependent caring for others is so unhealthy, your next step is to consciously decide to receive your own caring.

**Opening to receive is a conscious decision.**

Our ability to receive fully has become disabled. Collateral damage from the ban on selfishness has been the silencing and deadening of receiving. When we got into the habit of over-focusing on others, we inadvertently shut down our own ability to experience receiving. Very few people know that the experience of receiving has any value at all.

**A closer look at giving and receiving.**

Prominent thoughts, such as "It is more blessed to give than it is to receive," have deterred many of us from receiving. Being less blessed to receive invites the receiver to feel somehow "less than" in value than the person who is in a position to give. Many of us feel so badly about the fact that we are in need, that we spiral down into a well of negative self-judgment: self pity, feeling trapped in helplessness and hopelessness, or believing there's something wrong with me.

A person might even feel that they are sinful when

beckoned to or needing to receive because, after all, what is the opposite of blessed? This is unfortunate because this concept actually devalues those in need, those who are in a position to really benefit from receiving.

Besides, isn't receiving the essential other side of giving? Where would the givers be if there were no receivers?

A corollary and mistaken belief of "It is more blessed to give than to receive" is that giving and receiving are mutually exclusive, meaning they cannot exist at the same time. As if when a person is giving, it is not possible to receive.

Even among people who consider themselves caring individuals, there has been a strong prohibition against receiving—religiously, humanitarianly, altruistically. Teachers, social workers, pastors, and many other professionals hold in their mind that it is taboo to think of themselves as gaining anything when working with their students and clients. I found this when I was teaching public-school teachers how to let go of resentment and to handle difficulties that they encountered in their professional relationships with students and parents. They were loathe to accept that they were also gaining anything while they helped their students learn. Even gaining appropriate satisfaction felt uncomfortable to them.

But in fact, they were gaining valuable growth experiences for their professional performance and their professional and personal conduct in life. Their concern was that they could be viewed as exploiting or gaining at the expense of their students, even though they were not gaining anything at the expense of their students. This belief, that a benefit gained or felt could only be gained at the student's expense, is a faulty belief. There is a huge, faulty belief system built upon this idea, which leaves teachers and other service professionals feeling exhausted, depleted, drained, and burned out.

As a result, many continue providing good service until that service deteriorates. At that point, either the deteriorating service continues or the professionals leave disgruntled, frustrated, and disappointed. Had they been able to recognize the ways they were receiving naturally, and not at anyone else's expense, they could have continually felt rejuvenated and re-energized. This ability to receive would have supported their own continued growth, development, and even healing.

The above words have healing energy for you, whether or not you have experienced the situations in the examples I've given.

> Reread those words about receiving, and do so with the intention of allowing the healing energy to wash in to you, healing subtle, faulty thoughts you have been carrying that you may not even be aware of.

When we habitually, inadvertently, ignorantly, and even nobly and conscientiously close off to receiving, we close off our access to our:

~ Wisest thinking

~ Ability to have compassionate detachment

~ Ultimate clarity of mind

~ Ultimate use of our feelings to inform our wisest decision making

In essence, we are closing off access to our Innate Inner Wise Self.

As you can see, your approach to receiving can have a huge impact on the Self-Care activities you undertake. Your attitude to receiving will determine whether or not you choose a Self-Care approach.

There has also been a growing boon over the last few decades in the area of self-help, which is directly related to Self-Care. There are more and more books like this one that encourage you to become your own wise adviser, to seek your best next-growth steps inside yourself. There are many, many uplifting, positive-growth programs and personal workshops to attend.

This is promising.

Before we move on, take a soft, full breath in, and relax your body, relax your mind.

# BREATHE

Allow yourself to feel the energy of this
reading washing, flowing through you, taking
any limiting feelings, thoughts, and beliefs out
of your body.

Feel the letting go that is taking place
through your reading experience.

Allow your being to absorb what you've
read. Any new information that you don't
take in at this point will be there in your
energy field whenever you need it.

## So what are the practicalities of Self-Care for me?

How have you been about receiving? Where are you at now?

Many people are shy and uncomfortable receiving. This shows up when they are faced with compliments, gifts, accolades, attention, or a need for help. Or it's not on their radar screen at all. They just don't think about it. They are likely to have never considered it. They may be totally focused on giving.

Another important factor in receiving is how often you wish others would think of you and your needs, likes, dislikes—at least a little consideration, please! There might have been times that you've been furious about this.

This is an indication that you are not receiving. Wanting others to meet your needs indicates that you have unmet needs. An example is that no matter how many times someone says you look great, you are so smart, you are a great mom, wife, daughter, etc., you don't feel that it's true. The caveat is that the only one who can meet your needs is you.

Most of us have become deadened to the experience of receiving. When we give, we might feel depleted, as if we are stripping ourselves and depleting ourselves even more. There's nothing to give when we have nothing. This means that you not only must take care of yourself first, you must continue to take care of yourself at the same time you take care of others.

## Practically speaking, what are the ways of Self-Care?

Let's first look at what you're letting go of—the outdated, obsolete methods—so you can notice inside yourself which ones seem familiar.

As mentioned earlier, we've all developed Self-Caring methods in childhood that helped us deal with the overpowering way the behavior of adults affected us. Our attitudes and behaviors ensured that we'd survive to adulthood. The difficulty is that these immaturely devised Self-Caring thoughts and behaviors have become habits.

One of the ways of Self-Care is to allow new information and new understandings to dislodge and propel counterproductive, habitual thinking and behavior to leave voluntarily.

Just considering this thought allows it to become so.

Allow this concept to work in this way, as we enumerate some of those immaturely devised Self-Caring behaviors. We'll bring them up to the surface for clearing. Think of them as coming forward, waving their hands and arms, seeking your attention, saying "Let me go...Let me go next. I want to go!"

Below is a list of immature and obsolete protections. *Please allow them to leave.* They desperately want to.

~ I don't want to get hurt again.

~ I'll keep my feelings to myself.

~ If I say how I really feel, they'll get angry with me and I can't allow that.

~ I'll keep my thoughts to myself.

~ I'll just be quiet and not rock the boat.

~ I'll just wait and they will come around.

~ If I drop hints, he/she will get the idea.

~ No one is really interested in what I think.

~ No one cares about me.

~ I'll just do this one more time, for them.

~ How can he/she hurt me this way?

~ If I don't focus on this, it will go away.

~ I wish they would disappear.

~ Doesn't anyone see how I'm suffering?

~ I'll just focus on something else.

~ If I focus on my work and taking care of the kids, that's all that matters.

~ All I do is take care of everyone else.

~ I can do it myself (when no one volunteers to assist you):

> clean up
>
> manage everything in regards to the children
>
> do things around the house
>
> handle the finances
>
> work outside the home *and* manage everything inside the home

~ I will do everything myself, with resentment.

~ It must be my fault.

~ Problems in the relationship must be my fault.

~ I'll take care of myself. I'll never let anyone know of my needs.

~ I'll never take care of myself, and they'll just have to figure it out.

~ I'll never let them know how much I hate them.

~ I'll show them. I'll be perfect in everything I do.

~ I believe that the other person really knows what my likes and dislikes are.

~ I believe that the other person knows what's meaningful to me.

~ What went on in my home when I was a child was probably what went on in every home.

~ Children should be seen and not heard.

~ I notice that I react in ways similar to my parent or caretaker of the same gender.

~ I notice that I react in ways opposite to the ways of my parent or caretaker of the same gender.

~ I model my behavior after the parent or caretaker I liked the most.

~ I can't do this.

~ This is too hard.

~ This is so hard.

~ They can do it much better than I can; it's best that I leave it to them.

There may be other thoughts, beliefs, behaviors, and attitudes that are eager to leave as well. They have been running your experience from their rooted home in your subconscious. As they leave, their energy becomes transmuted into benign energy that's available to us all for creativity. Thank you for choosing to let go.

Now let's look at another aspect of Self-Care.

**Self-Caring is constructive, growth-propelling, life-satisfaction-inducing, awareness-providing, and choice-expanding.**

How does Self-Care accomplish all of this? Check out the following list, which is by no means complete:

- ~ Slowing down your experiencing

- ~ Gathering information from your feelings

- ~ Hearing a kernel of truth in what others are saying to you or about you, even when you dislike what's being said

- ~ Sensing your feelings with specificity

- ~ Sensing your emotional boundaries

- ~ Speaking up when your boundaries are crossed

- ~ Informing others of your boundaries as they get close to crossing them

- ~ Sensing any uh-oh feelings

~ Saying *No, thank you*

~ Saying *No, thank you* guilt-free

~ Receiving while you are giving

~ Hearing (aloud and in your head) the words you use:

    toward or about yourself

    toward or about others

~ Observing yourself

~ Instituting boundaries

~ Owning the belief that all of you is under your jurisdiction

~ Owning the belief that only you are under your jurisdiction

~ Allowing yourself to spend time letting the fitting words come to you for any communications

Stop a moment and take out a piece of paper. List all the feelings you'd like to experience—don't hold back.

Call each feeling into the room one at a time, allowing yourself to breathe each feeling in with the air. Into your lungs, into your blood, then circulating throughout all systems, organs, cells, and atoms in your body...even to the point of radiating out, through, and beyond your body and into your energy field. Repeat this process for each feeling on your list, taking as much time as you need.

This is a great point to stop so you can appreciate yourself and how far you have come since the beginning of Step One, as well as your openness and willingness to improve your life with ease.

You have taken in much new information and have allowed a validation and reorganization of what you have stored within.

Take a rest now. When you resume, you'll relax as I share several stories which show how applying these Self-Care methods can play out in everyday life.

REST

# Life Experiences

# CHAPTER SIX

# The New Me Debuts in Relationships

## How I'm Different and How I'm the Same

You have received an abundance of new information and thoughts from this book. Now I would like to share and explain how I used this same knowledge to gain freedom in my relationships.

Let's begin by opening to receive insight into possibilities you may never have dreamed possible in your relationships.

Start by tightening both fists, inhaling as you hold them for the count of five, and then as you open them, slowly exhale, relaxing and opening to receive.

Now bring up in your mind a relationship you are currently in that:

~ is in need of help

~ you are fed up with

~ has exhausted its usefulness

~ needs to be traded in

~ infuriates you

~ disappoints you

~ needs refurbishing

~ needs evacuating

~ needs clearing

~ needs healing

~ upsets you

~ others criticize you about

~ has you feeling in a rut or stuck

~ you know is counterproductive

~ you want to change and can't

~ you feel guilty about

~ you have shame about

~ you hate yourself for

~ you judge yourself about

~ is like the same old negative thing over again

Any one of these issues is fine. As I tell you my story, keep your situation in the back of your mind.

But before we do that, I'm going to show you a temporary way of "viewing" the situation you've brought to mind: it will get you started on considering your own new ways of seeing yourself and others in your situation. A new perspective.

Pretend that you are watching a movie, and you are an actor in the movie. This is tapping into the you who can witness what is going on in your life, the observing you. In this movie, you are both the participant and the observer—yes, you have a dual focus. You can do this. You have a fine mind with the capability to look into yourself and your situation in this way. This may be a hidden talent that you didn't know you had. If so, guess what?

You have many other hidden talents, and your increasing awareness will continue to reveal these expanding talents and abilities.

Skip back to the movie approach to viewing your life. Allow all of the following elements of moviemaking to be present, and try to notice:

~ yourself as the star

~ others as supporting actors

~ the lighting—who or what is highlighted

~ the angle of the viewing—who and what is small or larger

~ the directing—who is directing

~ the insistence that the script be adhered to

~ the flexibility or inflexibility of the director

~ the location of the stage

~ the arena

~ the expressions on the characters' faces

~ the different ways the roles can be played

~ the nature of the characters

~ humor—the introduction of

~ extreme drama

~ the lighting—more light, less light

~ the volume of the sounds

~ the types of sounds

~ background music—introducing some

~ are there actors who play several parts?

~ how are all the actors expressing
  aspects of you?

~ your private dialogues with the characters

~ your private dialogues with inanimate objects
  and props

~ the speed of the playback or replay

Not only can you watch all aspects of the movie, you have the ability to slow down the speed so you can see even more.

Imagine yourself as reporting from the inside. Close your eyes and access the speed-control dial within you.

Bring to mind a simple situation in which you were rushing, or maybe you felt rushed by someone else. Now, as if you are in the control booth watching the scene on a screen, use the dial to slow down the movement in the scene so you can notice the steps you were taking in the situation.

Now speed it up again, then slow it down again. Feel your ability to control the pace.

The speed-control dial can also be used effectively in current situations to help you really appreciate many elements that are present in each moment of your inner and outer life.

The movie approach, the speed-dial control, and trying on the perspectives offered in this and previous chapters all helped me to gradually become more and more conscious that I was *really* taking myself on a journey while living through the story that unfolds below.

The curtain's going up…

We started out as high school boyfriend and girlfriend. When I was eighteen, there was one special guy who held me throughout my father's death and all the weeks that followed, even though I was going out with other guys at the time. I felt totally safe in this young man's arms and totally bonded to him. The other guys all faded from view.

My mother was a non-stop talker, so I never had a chance to become friendly with silence, although I thirsted for it. I experienced him as quiet and reveled in it, even though my mother said, "He's too quiet for you."

After he graduated college, we married. I loved being married. We had fun, no real responsibility other than our jobs, and we enjoyed friends, outings, vacations, and being married.

Four years into the marriage, I returned to college. In our seventh year, I emerged from school with a master's degree in social work. But our relationship suffered because I had directed so much focus, energy, and time on my schoolwork. I suppose the good thing in the long run was that my self-awareness had been ignited in a health-oriented way, although that was just the beginning and has felt like a very slow work-in-progress throughout many years.

Once I had a beginning awareness and some perspec-
tive of me, I could see more clearly—although still as if
through thick glasses—certain aspects to our relationship.
For example, I did most of the talking in the relation-
ship. I'm sure I had an inkling of an uh-oh feeling when
I realized this, but the feeling was faint, so I overrode it.
(I knew nothing in those days about my Inner Guide or
Inner Wisdom.)

As time went on, we continued our enjoyable activities.
As I developed, I grew in my work life and emotionally
lived in that safe cocoon within myself in my husband's
arms. My work life revolved around helping people get in
touch with and express their feelings as part of learning an
effective problem-solving approach in and to their lives. As I
was teaching this approach, I was living it for myself as well.

Our relationship often frustrated me because I'd ask my
husband what he felt about this or that, and he really
couldn't answer. He'd say, "What do you mean?" I knew
of no other words at the time to be more explicit, and I
said so. Dismay and frustration registered in me. I even
took his not answering (his "quietness") very personally,

as if he was holding back from me. Each time he couldn't answer me, a slowly mounting negativity toward him built inside me.

It never occurred to me to focus with gratitude on his love for me or his enjoyment of doing things for me and helping me with this or that. Feelings follow thoughts. Had I been able to shift my thinking, my feelings would have shifted and I would have been having a different and more satisfying experience—with likely no mounting negativity. Even now, I can hear one of my mother's quips, "live and learn!"

There were many other things going on in our life together that I enjoyed and so, as my mother used to say about me, I went along my merry way.

I still loved being together with my man—that old, wonderful, safe, and loving feeling. What I can see now as I look back is that *I loved how I felt*. I did not know that I was giving myself these feelings, that they were located within me and not being given to me by my husband. I thought he made me feel safe. His sweetness and kindness and love called up, or triggered, these feelings in me. The few times my focus unconsciously shifted to this aspect of our togetherness, I felt great. I was on automatic. I had no conscious awareness that this great feeling came from within.

A year after I received my master's degree, we purchased a house and became busy with all the responsibilities that go along with that. We were great housemates, and we loved each other, problem-solved well together, and enjoyed friends and family together. We were the most compatible couple we had ever heard of.

A year or two later, in addition to my nine-to-five agency job, I started working two to three evenings a week to build an independent, private practice so I could eventually work part-time from home whenever we would have a child.

My husband and I worked as full partners in all areas of our lives except the sharing-of-feelings area. I used the language of feelings more and more and, to me, my husband appeared to speak less and less. While my "talking" toned down quite a bit, I noticed he still didn't volunteer any information about himself.

I now know that my Inner Wise Self kept bringing my attention back to this issue. In my mind, I'd toss this concern away, chalking it up to the differences in the way men and women communicate. Besides, I would check inside and all votes within me confirmed my love for this man and my love for being with him.

So what was the problem?

Four years later, in the twelfth year of our marriage, we gave birth to our child. We were steeped together, sharing in the many joys, high points, low points, and challenges, and participating in and supporting the care for and growth of our little one.

If you are a feelings-sensitive individual, you may know how nice it would have been to confer with my partner on a feelings level during many of the experiences I've described so far. I had no conscious idea how my thirst for this was increasing as time went on and life situations increased in complexity. I was not aware that I had unmet needs that were growing. I was swimming to keep up with the current day-to-day life experiences. Despite my working to expand my self-awareness in hopes of feeling better—a goal still in its early phases and quite imma-ture—my caring for others overgrew the garden of my focus on myself. My devotion to others had totally blotted out from my view any light from my Innate Inner Wisdom, and my observing self had not yet been developed.

How useful it would have been to observe myself in the totality of the situation. It would have been great to see what was going on and to notice if I wanted to change my perspective on anything; if so, I would have appreciated more of what was happening. Knowing I had a choice about how to look at things could have connected me with the feeling of control over my life.

As time went on, our compatibility shined through in our parenting as well. Many times our son said, "Can't you guys get together and say things once? I hear the same thing from both of you." Funny thing was, we didn't plan that. At intervals during the day we sometimes compared notes to find that, independently, we had expressed the same thought with exactly the same words to our son. It was a little freaky.

But from my limited perspective, the gulf between us grew. I felt isolated and alone. I had an inkling that much of my experience was my responsibility (*aha!* my Innate Inner Wisdom), so I went to therapy to sort myself out from the blame I felt toward my husband. I remember a moment when I realized the exact words I needed to say to him for me to own my responsibility and to cite his responsibility for his part. I felt I could no longer play both emotional parts in the relationship: my own part, and second-guessing or trying to figure out or simply assuming what he was feeling.

I was coming to an end of a phase of my codependent caretaking in our relationship. I had been in the habit of completely coordinating our lives, including doing all the talking. I was an excellent coordinator with a huge dose of resentment.

"Hindsight is 20/20," my mother used to say.

### *The benefit of hindsight is to file the learning for future use.*

Good to know. But unfortunately I didn't have that hindsight then.

One day I came home and said, "Honey, I cannot go another day without having us both share from our hearts. I'm not sure what else there is, but I just know I can't go on together with you like this."

And he said, "You mean, even though we love each other, and we've been together for years? Even though we enjoy being in the same house? Even though we are good parents together?"

"Yes."

There was a very uncomfortable silence. I knew that I was taking care of myself in a way I couldn't ever have done before.

Thus started the beginning of our separating, our ultimate divorce, and the start of a relationship I could love.

He was in shock and so couldn't participate in the coordinating or details of this new phase of our life together. I, however, had already worked through all resentment about many things. In fact, I had been working on letting go of resentment, anger, and fear. I did this by learning *Centering in My Self* and *Appreciating Myself* and *My Life as a Work of Art*. I was learning to take care of myself with a healthy respect for the kernel of truth in others' opinions. I ditched the codependent and dysfunctional preoccupation with the need to believe others' negative opinions.

Still new at evaluating my growth, I was surprised to find that when I gently helped my husband take steps to be on his own, I had neither anger nor resentment. I really had grown. This was something new to appreciate in the portrait of my self. I was able to use my coordinating skills to guide us out of that marriage and into new lives. This time, coordinating was healthy and healing and not controlling, laced with anger, resentment, and codependence.

I checked with my husband to see where he was on using attorneys or mediators, and if we both wanted me to seek out the professionals who would assist us. I also assisted him while he was looking for an apartment. While doing this, I was sensitive to how much he could or felt like he could do on his own.

There are many ways people can go through this experience, and this is only one way. You may read things in this story that you disagree with or feel uncomfortable with. Keep an open mind to the lessons that you can receive; they might show you how to own your ways of doing things. Remember that your Innate Inner Wise Voice will help you experience your situations in your best way possible.

My love for my husband was still intact. It cushioned my every expression and act of assistance. I resisted every temptation to declare what would be my choice for his new life. This meant that I was at my own center and the star in my life. His life and choices did not have to revolve around me.

I now realize that being the controlling (i.e., talking too much) wifey-type star in my husband's life wasn't giving me the sense of connection and intimacy that I desired down deep. These were the emotional needs that I was looking for him to meet. I didn't know that I wasn't open to receiving and that it was up to me to access what I would need to meet these needs.

It dawned on me that there was a real possibility that my soon-to-be-former husband could decide to want no part of me in his new life. With this thought in mind, I asked him if I could be in on his sharing about our breakup with his brother and sister-in-law.

"Sure," he said. I was thrilled because I love these people. So I followed my Inner Wise Voice into shaky territory and told them I still wanted to be part of their lives and the lives of their children. Let me specific: I requested continued invitations to all holiday dinners, birthdays, and family events.

Not only did I love these people, I had a son who was part of this family and I wanted to continue sharing this closeness with him and all of them as long as I could.

The shaky territory was that I could have been viewed as the stereotypical, evil ex-wife that they wouldn't want to have around. I was pleasantly surprised when they said, "Sure, that would be great."

**When fear stops you from hearing your Inner Wise Voice, you miss opportunities to get your needs met.**

Sure, I could have let fear stop me from asking my in-laws that question, but I've never regretted facing up to that fear and doing it anyway. Consequently, I learned that following my Inner Wise Voice can lead to pleasant surprises.

My husband took an apartment about two miles from the house. We settled into a new routine. It may seem strange, but in reality the closeness we shared did continue. At one point, he told me he was upset that our fifteen-year-old son never called him. Having the perspective of knowing and loving both of them, my Inner Self gave me the words. "The parent is the leader in the parent-child relationship. So you might want to call frequently and plan regular get-togethers with him." We were still good co-parents and he often came over to visit with our son.

After a while I felt a desire to share more time with my soon-to-be-former husband. He had Tuesdays and Wednesdays off from work. Following the whispers of my Inner Wise Voice, I asked if he was interested in spending some time together. He was open to it and we started to run our errands together and have a lunch or dinner together each week. This was an enjoyable way to be together.

During this time, my observing self helped me see subtle differences in my reactions to our everyday life. For instance, I realized that I had no responsibility for his household needs. I didn't worry if his dishes were clean or if his laundry was done. This was so enlightening to me and a welcome surprise. I was realizing that my perspective had more to do with my upset than I had thought. I started to see that the props and actors were in new places and in new relationship to one another. We were the same people but now playing our roles differently.

I also discovered the speed-control dial for slowing things down and to see and appreciate more nuances of what was occurring.

Once I slowed things down, I saw that since we were no longer 24/7 under the same roof, I no longer looked to him to satisfy my emotional needs. I stopped caring that he was not conversant in his feelings. Men typically do not share feelings, but while we lived together, I never let him off the hook on that. How amazing, I decided, that it no longer bothered me. This was no small lesson.

My perspective was changing; my mind was opening.

I wondered what else wouldn't bother me. Time went by and I collected more treasures of awareness, like not caring about his household needs. Another treasure was that there was no longer any pressure about anything in our relationship. There were no longer any have-tos. I simply enjoyed being with him. I still did not know if at some point he might not want me as part of his life. I realized I was caring for myself by letting go of my concern about him not wanting me or him not being able to meet my needs. My happiness was to be found within me.

There were many more enlightenments. He told me in retrospect that he had realized he heard his mother's voice every time I opened my mouth. This was music to my ears. Someone else might have been insulted but, at this point, I had studied the ideas presented in this book and was trying to put them into practice. With the geographic space created between us, I could hear these things that I would not have heard had we continued under the same roof.

This became our life for the next five and a half years. It was enjoyable and enlightening.

And then a couple of things happened. I sold my house and was considering moving in temporarily with one of my girlfriends. I thought this would be fun. I actually had three friends I considered living with but their extra spaces were occupied with other visitors. I could have felt this was quite disappointing but yet, in reality, it opened up other possibilities.

To my surprise, my former husband said, "You could always come here."

"Really?" I said with reserve. Inside, however, I felt, *Gee, that could be nice.*

And then an uh-oh feeling came up. What if I slipped back into my old ways? I figured I'd better say something to him about this concern. This was my Inner Wisdom guiding me to take care of me in another new way.

So I did. I shared this concern, and a brilliant gem of a treasure was revealed. Out of his mouth came, "Yes, I have the same concern about myself. We'd have to let each other know whenever that would come up."

We then agreed to put any concern or fear on the table and to handle it jointly. We did have to consciously focus together but it was easier than we had thought.

I decided to try moving in with him.

Right about this same time, our son called to say he was staying permanently in his college town, and he wanted to know if I thought either his dad or I would ever consider moving there. I knew right away that I was going.

I turned to his father to float the idea. And he said that he was interested too. I felt a flutter of excitement. I was moving to a new state…with this man? All of a sudden, nothing was like it ever was before.

Having recovered from hearing his mother's voice come out of my mouth, he gained a new perspective. When I realized this, I also realized that he was still a man of few words but I noticed that what he did say was very rich and full of meaning. I wonder if that had always been true.

I often noticed the same issues crop up that we had had in the past, but they looked different to me, and I was not bothered. This was a result of living the ideas covered in Steps One through Five as outlined in this book.

I did a lot of work with my new ability to step back from situations and use the speed-control dial to get a better look at what was happening. I used the dial to slow things down so that I could choose the responses I wanted to offer. This was very different from how I had been before. Now, it was as if I had become a new person.

So we moved to a new state. And after about a year in our new apartment, we decided to remarry. Now, I have all the things I loved about our original marriage and none of the things I didn't love. And the joy continues to unfold as our lives keep getting better and better.

# CHAPTER SEVEN

## The New Me Faces Life's Challenging Situations

*An Adventure in How I'm Different*

What you are about to read next is one person's experience—mine. You, or anyone else for that matter, might experience it in a different way. As you have read in earlier chapters, there are as many ways to experience a situation as there are people who look at it. Even with all other factors being equal—the same childhood drawbacks and societal influences, for example—we each bring to the shared experience our own unique perspective.

What I did have to my advantage was an understanding of the approaches we covered in this book's first five chapters: Centering in My Self, Appreciating Me and My Life as a Work of Art, Hearing My Inner Wisdom, Honoring My Self, and Caring for My Self. These tools are advantageous for improving your ability to be happy, no matter what, in any situation you find yourself in, and they were particularly helpful to me in my experience.

When you're open to receiving—when you see, hear, or sense how another person experiences things—your mind opens and expands way beyond only your experience. You are then able to automatically view your own situation from many different angles, and sometimes all at once. I say this in order to invite you to relax as you read the following story of how I went through a challenging situation...also known as a life crisis.

## Life can change in an instant.

In July of 1993, it had been one and a half months since I had been elected to the school board. I was feeling somewhat disappointed because I had sought this position in order to make a difference and to participate in something stimulating—yet there was nothing going on. We were meeting monthly instead of twice a month, and with no committee meetings, it was dull, dull, dull.

One day, I felt particularly disappointed about the school board experience and how I was viewing it in that moment. I thought to myself, "I'd like a situation that would accelerate my growth and through which I could feel my feelings more deeply." I had thought the school board experience would do this for me. Why did I think that? After all, the school board experience had come in response to a different request of the Universe—one that I had about making a difference and participating in something stimulating—and not something that would accelerate my growth and through which I could feel my feelings more deeply.

It's best to be specific, I've learned.

"Okay," I thought, "I'll ask the Universe for this again," because the school board experience was obviously not

doing "it" for me. A little niggling thought tagged along
with the first one: "And I'd prefer to live through it, rather
than die through it."

This thought popped into my head, seemingly automatically, but I knew where it had come from. A teacher of
mine, June, used to say, "Watch what you ask for; you
just might get it!" It was a great thing, that life-over-death
qualifier that popped into my head, as if I had nothing to do with it. But I left it at that, and didn't give it
another thought.

When September came, I realized that school board
business is typically minimal during the summer because
things picked up quite a bit when the school year
started. I decided the election and board position were
an excellent response to what I had originally asked for:
"To get actively involved in making a positive difference
in people's lives and to participate in something interesting and stimulating."

It all seems really obvious to me now, but during that
summer I didn't have even a flash of a thought that I could

still receive what I had asked for. I didn't have the awareness to know that patience was called for, that I needed
to await the full bloom on the flower of my request.

All of this was, at that point, *outside of my awareness.*

As the year went on, I loved the school board experience. It was more than I could have ever asked for: being
on an educational lay team of mixed professionals who
were all focused on the well-being of 3,000 children,
16,000 taxpayers, plus parents and staff. What a great
opportunity for contribution and personal development.

But in late March of the following year—in a different
arena of my life—I was told, "There is an irregularity in
your routine mammogram. In these situations we usually
recommend a biopsy. Don't worry—it may be nothing."

My first thought was, "Oh, this is the situation I asked
for—the accelerating growth experience through which
I can feel my feelings more deeply. Wow, good thing I
added 'and I'd prefer to live through it rather than die
through it.'"

I also thought how curious it was that I was calm inside. I suppose on some level I really believed I would live through this life crisis.

I set an appointment with a surgeon and took with me a friend, who said, "It's probably nothing. I've had many of those micro-calcifications and they watch them and that's it." I figured she'd be a good support person to bring along.

The doctor looked me straight in the eye and said, "There's a 15 percent chance that this is cancerous." He explained that it could be nothing or it could be something. And if it's something, he added, looking at me closely, "You know what this is, and it could require surgery. The removal of the breast."

My friend gasped, but she didn't make a sound.

"Where are my feelings?" I wondered.

I looked him back, straight in the eye, and said, "Look, if you have to take one, you might as well take two. I'm not coming back." Where had these particular words come from? In retrospect, I know they came from somewhere in my gut—my Innate Inner Wisdom.

He said, "We don't like to take healthy tissue."

But I knew in my gut that if I had one pre-fab breast and one natural breast, I would be in therapy three times a week for fifteen years. How did I know myself so well? I knew that there would be thousands of thoughts consuming my attention and that would be triggered when I looked in the mirror each day: seeing two different-looking breasts, and then having fears and other thoughts associated with redoing the whole ordeal if I should need to have the other breast removed.

Friends and clients who have had one breast removed have shared these kinds of thoughts with me over the years. My guess is that I, too, was subject to having some, if not all, of those same thoughts. I was not willing to go forward in my life and be focused in that way.

"Well," I responded to the doctor, "I worked with a psychiatrist for several years, and I'll get a note from him validating the truth of why removing both breasts would be preferable." I was glad I had that truth in my pocket to whip out now when I needed it, but I also wondered if I would be able to find the psychiatrist, since it had been years since I'd seen him.

Continuing his support of not having unnecessary surgery, the doctor said, "Well, if you do have breast cancer, there's only a 10 percent chance that it would occur in the other breast."

Brazenly, I said, "Doctor, if I have breast cancer in one breast where you've said I only have a 15 percent chance, that's 100 percent for me. So 10 percent would mean nothing to me because I already have it 100 percent."

The doctor responded, "All right, all right, we'll do it."

My forthrightness, I realized later, was me following my Inner Wise Voice.

As my friend and I left the doctor's office, I saw that she still appeared dumbstruck and in shock. She was astounded by the severity of the conversation, the fact that I could be dealing with cancer, and how it was so starkly discussed. My hunch was that while witnessing my situation, she came face to face with her fears and feelings about her own situation, which was being monitored by this very same doctor.

I shifted right away out of Self-Caring and into caretaker mode to focus on my friend. I was helping her manage her scared feelings. I reflected that this could be a good thing for me to do, or not. Either way, it certainly took my mind off my own situation.

Later that day, I arranged for the biopsy. I frequently checked on my feelings and I felt fine. I shared with another friend, Karen, the date I planned to go to the pre-op visit and she asked who was going with me.

"No one," I said.

She said, "Ellen, if it were me, would you allow me to go by myself?"

She was right. I knew I wouldn't have allowed her to go without support.

She continued, "Don't you think you're having some feelings about this that may surface or erupt during the pre-op experience?"

Her questions made me realize that I wasn't taking care of myself. She was reminding me that most of what goes on inside us is below the surface of the 7 percent wide awake, daytime consciousness. The part below the surface comes up at anytime in the form of uncontrolled reactions and behaviors triggered by happenings around us and by our own internal attitudes or thoughts.

I also had a flash of thought that I had asked for an experience to accelerate my growth and to help me feel my feelings more deeply. And I realized at that moment I wasn't in touch with any feelings at all.

I asked my husband to come with me and he did. I was aware enough to be watching for my feelings when I was at the hospital, and I was mentally present for the pre-op testing. I wasn't really scared. I was a little annoyed at the inconvenience and I was a bit critical of the process. Where were my emotions? Still under wraps.

The next ten days were unexpectedly intense. I figured that since I knew I was going to live, I'd just go about my business. I believed I would have an easier time of waiting for the results of the biopsy if I just focused on my everyday life. That's called rationalization or denial. They're wonderfully protective, Self-Caring mechanisms that came on automatically to protect me from feelings that might be too intense for me to handle.

Except, I really wanted to feel my feeling more deeply, and now I was not feeling them at all. I was aware of this. This was somewhat understandable because when things became overwhelming as a child, I learned this protective mechanism.

But once I became aware of the "not feeling" protective mechanism, its cover was blown. I really did want to feel, which I understood was a doorway to making conscious choices in life. What I was not aware of, I couldn't change. I knew this and very much wanted awareness.

Gradually I recognized that my new medical situation took up my entire focus and consumed my every waking thought. I kept saying to myself, "I know I'm going to live, so what's all this preoccupation?" I had thoughts like, "What if this requesting your experience is a bunch of bull?" and "What if I'm wrong?" And the word *cancer* replayed in my mind, over and over again. I also had thoughts of chemotherapy and dying, although they were way in the background.

a h h h h ...I couldn't get these and many other thoughts out of my mind. Who was I kidding? I wasn't calm at all at this point.

My next best approach was to distract myself. I scheduled us to attend several Broadway shows. These were shows that I loved and was looking forward to seeing. At the theatre, I noticed that I strained to stay focused on the shows. Now I was feeling strain in my head and even some jumpiness in my chest—anxiety. Forget the shows. I don't even know what they were about.

Fortunately, I was able to reflect on what I was experiencing. This was my observer self. I tried breathing consciously because it had been recommended to me. I wasn't too good at that. My only course of action at that point was to weather the experience and wait for the biopsy results.

A few days later, the doctor's office called and asked me to come in to hear the results of the biopsy. My first thought was, "That's really good that they don't give it out over the phone." I set the appointment and planned to bring my husband and my friend of longest standing and my Self-Care conscience, Karen.

I wanted to be prepared so I went to the library. I found a great book that described in very short paragraphs the different types of cancer, stages, etc. Sitting at my kitchen table, minutes before we left for the doctor's office, I said, "I want to read out loud to the three of us about the different types of cancer so we'll know what the doctor is talking about if he says I have cancer."

They agreed and in two minutes I read the brief summaries. This was as far as I was willing to go into the future with my thoughts. I had been practicing "staying in the moment" and "not prewriting the script" of the scenes of my life.

## STAYING IN THE MOMENT

*Staying in the moment is a valuable skill for anyone to master. Actually moving forward out of the present moment saps you of precious energy. It may even be the reason so many people are plagued with fatigue and boredom. Staying in the moment allows you to trust that whatever occurs, you will have the feelings that fit that situation should it arrive. It is also important not to prewrite the script. You don't need to prematurely have the feelings. You may not need to have them at all, because alternate situations may arise calling for other feelings. You can learn to do this too. Keep practicing. It really pays off!*

Living in the moment was really paying off for me because I came to the appointment prepared, yet not expecting the worst.

The doctor came in and I saw he didn't have a smile on his face. All I remember hearing him say was the name of the cancer with the least negative consequences, based on the paragraph I'd read to the three of us.

"That's the one where I don't need chemo or radiation? And I'm going to live! We just have to remove it? So I only need surgery?"

He confirmed this with a nod. I was ecstatic that I was going to live. I jumped up from the table to give him a hug.

Karen was crying and my husband, who had been leaning against the wall, was sliding to the floor as he was passing out. They both had only heard *cancer*. They were focused on cancer and surgery. I was ecstatically focused on life. We were each having our own experiences while being all together.

The doctor said to my husband, "Snap out of it. I can only take care of one patient at a time." He snapped out of it.

I was amazed at the dynamics and interplay between

the characters, the lines we were saying, and the ways we were playing our parts, including me. It was so interesting to me.

This is a good point to stop reading.

Take a full breath and let it out slowly.

BREATHE

Sit quietly for a bit, reflect
on your own situations, and
how you can view them
differently now.

∽ LET'S CONTINUE

I asked the doctor if this was an emergency. It was not.
I could attend our son's fifth-grade graduation, go to
Montauk for our yearly vacation at the end of the school
year, and schedule the surgery for June 29.

I had three months before the surgery. For me, an
additional positive was that the surgeon agreed to do the
double mastectomy, although many people would not
agree. For me, the double mastectomy was a great thing,
but for someone else, it could be the worst thing.

Here's a thought I want you to really consider:

Make whatever is happening in your life work for you!
See it as being perfectly designed for your unique
growth needs.

As you learned to do in the previous chapters:

Look at your life as if through a magnifying glass to see
positives embedded in what seems like a
lousy situation.

Ask yourself, "What is the lesson in this for me?" even
if the answer doesn't come just then.

And then ask, "What are the other lessons in this for me?"

Also ask (perhaps to the Universe?), "Show me just
one other way to see this."

Say to yourself, "I can see this in a new way."

Consider that seeing it in one new way actually opens
the door to see many new ways.

During the three months before the surgery, I kept busy.

Even though my doctor's staff and the other attending staff had great track records for this surgery and came highly recommended, I knew things could go wrong. People make mistakes, and there was a chance that I wouldn't wake up from the surgery.

I wrote good-bye notes, sealed them in envelopes, and gave them to my husband, should they need to be opened. I did this just in case my belief in qualifying my original request "to live through" my learning experience was unfounded. I guess I was covering all bases.

I focused on my intention to live in the moment and to make the most out of the months, weeks, and days before the surgery.

The hard thing about that weekend in Montauk was that I kept thinking, "these are my last days with my nipples," which I really loved. The fun my husband and I had had with them would never be the same again. I also thought, "Well, of all my body parts to give up, giving up my breasts and nipples would be my choice as a good trade for continued life." I refocused diligently over that weekend to make the most of every beautiful moment available by the ocean with my husband and my son.

Karen asked me if I minded her coming along to wait with my husband during the surgery. She was a dear to offer. I had learned much about Self-Care from her over the years so I paid close attention to the things that she said. Karen's idea interested me. We both felt that my husband might benefit from support. The additional benefit was that if my husband needed support in advocating for me while I was in the hospital, Karen could step in. It's wise to have a person with you in this kind of a situation; they can advocate for you should you need it. This is a form of Self-Care. These ideas may be new to you, but please recognize the practical, resourceful nature of this information for yourself and those you know.

It turns out my husband was glad that we had this plan.

Karen then mentioned coming into the pre-op room with me. I said I thought the hospital wouldn't allow it. She smiled and said, "That may be true, so what?"

Now finally aware of the undulations of emotion rumbling beneath my surface, I figured I probably couldn't speak up if I needed or wanted something. I welcomed her self-assured presence. That kind of advocate suits me just fine.

The curtain rises on the morning of the surgery...

The hospital staff told us that Karen was not permitted to accompany me into the pre-op room. Karen gently and directly looked into the eyes of the nurse and says, "If she were a child, she'd have a parent with her. She's having many feelings and has fears; you are a fine nurse and you understand that. And I won't be a bother, I'm here to be a support."

The nurse agreed.

While in pre-op, I said to Karen, "I'm cold. I wish I had a blanket."

"No problem," she said, "I'll ask the nurse."

The nurse's response was a bit of a surprise. "Sorry, we don't have any."

I could sense Karen's energy coming up from her feet. She looked the nurse in the eye and softly said, "This is a hospital and you and I know that there are blankets. My friend is cold. Could you please get her a blanket?"

Within five minutes I had a warmed blanket and another if I needed it. I was so happy Karen was with me because I would never have had the strength to respond to the nurse's "no." And I would have been freezing and very upset. It's cold in pre-op rooms, so who wouldn't want a blanket? A warm one.

The anesthesiologist came in next. I was able to speak up to ask that no sedative—or anything, for that matter—be given to me until I was ready. Years before, while giving birth to our son by caesarean, a sedative was put in my IV without my knowledge. There were things I needed to say but I couldn't move my mouth to speak. That infuriated me and so I was clear that this time, I would do what I could to be able to voice my thoughts. That Inner Wise Voice was getting stronger. I was glad I could speak up about this and my wishes were respected.

*Self-Care. Self-Care. Self-Care.*

I thanked Karen as they wheeled me into the operating room. She said, "We'll see you when you get to recovery."

"How will you ever be able to do that?"

She said, "Don't worry, we will."

In the operating room, I asked if the team liked working together. They all smiled affirmatively at me and at each other. I also asked if any of them had been drinking late the night before, was anyone hung over? They said no.

It felt good in there. Then I thought, *G-d, if you are there, it's been a great life. If it has to end today, I'm satisfied. Thank you so much.*

I said to the medical team, "Okay, I'm ready."

As if in *no time*, I felt a warmth around me. A soothing, lovely warmth. I slowly opened my eyes in what felt like a lovely awakening. I glanced ahead, saw a clock, and the time registered in my mind. The awakening almost felt womb-like, yet I was awake in the recovery room. I was so happy that I had awakened. Delighted, actually.

After a nurse came over to greet me, she answered my question about the lovely warmth. I was in a lightweight, inflated, warm-air paper blanket. Someone said later that these are given to counter drops in blood pressure, common during surgery. The blanket was a lovely touch to the awakening experience. Thank you, dropping blood pressure.

Within only a few minutes, I heard my name spoken very softly. I had a direct view to the swinging doors of the recovery room, and I saw two faces, my husband and Karen, peeking in.

"Hi. You did great. We're going to get something to eat and we'll see you a little later."

It triggered wonderful feelings of security, personal value, feeling cared about, and comfort. Gratitude welled up in me like never before.

I figured it was time to test my body and see what was going on. I found that I couldn't move my body or my limbs, but I could turn my head. I was really tired. Somehow I just surrendered to the restfulness of not moving. I rested in my body for at least the next twenty-four hours.

When I graduated from the recovery room and went to a regular hospital room, I heard myself describe my immobility as if I had been hit by a truck—not smashed, just immobile. My husband was sweet and caring as he fed me ice chips and later ices. I couldn't lift even a finger. Although I was not in any pain, I could barely talk. Karen helped me ask my husband if he would investigate sleeping over in the hospital with me. The hospital agreed to it and provided a cot. It was so great to have his presence and attention there overnight.

In the middle of the night, at what felt like about 3:00 a.m., the doctor came in and awakened me. He whispered, "We just got back the pathology report, and you were right. There were pre-cancerous cells in your other breast. That was a great idea to remove it."

Wow. That was really *a great validation for appreciating, listening to, and honoring my Inner Wise Self.*

All of which were important steps in Caring for My Self to the nth degree!

I still felt the original ecstasy I'd had, and now a euphoria started in as well. **The more value I saw in each situation, the better I felt about the entire experience.**

I was really building up a euphoric head of steam, in part through other remarkable key moments, learnings, awarenesses, and revelations such as these:

A morning or two after the surgery, the plastic surgeon sitting at the end of the bed said, "You'll see...after you leave the hospital, this experience will shrink further and further into the past until it becomes a tiny speck, unrecognizable in the distance." I listened as he said his lines. They were beautiful. I recognized the value of what he was saying.

Over the next few months, my husband accompanied me to the plastic surgeon's office weekly. The doctor gradually added water to the expandable implants in order for my skin to expand to eventually accommodate the final size implants.

An interesting scene was the one in which the doctor brought up the question of size, since we could make my new breasts any size. The two men were discussing a C-cup size.

I couldn't believe that they were trying to convince me to have bigger breasts, so I interrupted them. "Guys, guys. I want a B-cup, which was my original size." Unless, of course, the doctor had some aesthetic or functional reason that bigger was better.

This was a very odd scene to be in. I really liked the doctor and felt great about his work, and I truly was in touch with loving my husband. I saw how comical this situation was and fully realized I was truly in charge of myself. And I was so grateful that I could speak up. Years before, I would have thought I was being discriminated against and that they were male chauvinist pigs. I was thrilled that I had outgrown feeling like a victim—of anything or anyone.

As a result, I was able to fully appreciate and enjoy the characters, roles, and the scene itself.

## Leaving behind victim consciousness frees you.

Another memorable moment was a few months later, when I got a nasty and cruel first call from a collection agency regarding monies that were my responsibility to pay and were beyond what the insurance company had covered.

As I listened to the caller, I felt a fire of fury come up within me. Then I got real calm and said, "Listen, I'm recovering from cancer and breast removal."

There was a long pause.

I continued, "I hope you never have to go through this. You are being mean and nasty to me, and after all I've been through. How about if I pay fifteen dollars a month until it's all paid up?"

"Okay," she said. How amazing was that! Another great performance by each actor.

In the weeks after the surgery, when I looked in the mirror with no top on, I saw two mounds of equal size. (Later they had artistically fashioned nipples made out of added skin.) I wondered how I knew I'd be okay with this?

Obviously all that self-revelation over the years added up to me seeing that my hunches about myself were accurate. Those hunches were the murmurs of the Inner Wise Voice I was learning to follow. **I could truly trust the Inner Wisdom that was left standing after limiting beliefs, thoughts, and feelings had been helped to leave.**

And one more thing. I never, ever liked wearing a bra. So there was a bonus—I never had to wear a bra ever again! I rode the tide of euphoria through all the experiences related to the mastectomy, reconstruction, and dealing with the responses of friends and relatives. That euphoria lasted approximately three years from its start. What a wonderful rush.

People said I handled things in a remarkable way and that I was brave and positive the whole time. They were amazed. Yet throughout it all, I was still conscious of the very real seriousness of the situation and events. However, I was able to be happy, no matter what, because I had learned and was actively practicing the principles and concepts in this book.

I truly believe that you can be happy no matter what the circumstances by finding and honoring your own way through the five steps to claim your own Inner Freedom.

PART IV

# Conclusion

*Looking at Yourself*
*through New Eyes*

Take a full breath and allow your body to relax.

Take another full breath and allow your mind to relax.

Calm and relaxed. Become calm and relaxed.

Open your mind to viewing the progress you have achieved in looking at yourself through new eyes.

**Toward a more centered you.**

When you started reading chapter one, you were searching. Did you know or even suspect that you were going to find a centered you? Probably not, because as you've now learned, so much comes from your childhood and popular-culture thinking that directs your attention away from yourself. The truth you've discovered is that you must be centered within yourself and your life in order to direct it and consciously create it. Without that centering, your unconscious does the creating, and leaves problem situations for you to undo and fix. Being centered positions you to wisely choose your behavior and expressions with an eye toward efficiency and effectiveness. The very fact that you read Step One, "Centering in My Self," allowed you to begin to integrate this idea. Congratulations!

## A starring role in a work of art.

You can expect the integration of centering in your self to continue and grow stronger as it anchors the steps that followed in chapters two through five. You've discovered that you are now centered as the star in your life. Giving yourself permission to be the star of your life opens your thinking to perceive your life as a work of art. Seeing yourself as a work of art allows you to view old, troublesome situations in new ways, giving them new meaning and value. You can see much more than when you originally lived through these experiences.

Self-judgment has been eliminated. You can now take pride in how you handled some things despite what you may have felt at the time. You're starting to see how situations can fit together to benefit you as learning experiences for your growth. Seeing yourself and your life as a work of art opens the doorway to feeling really good about yourself. This ripens you to consciously take on the role of the creative artist in your new, self-appreciating life. As your own creative artist, you get to paint pictures with new attitudes, feelings, and behaviors, and leave out the old dysfunctional thoughts, feelings, beliefs, and behaviors. This is the ability to live life from a new perspective.

## Hear your Innate Inner Wisdom.

Your centered focus—together with your new ability to value all of your many and varied colors, tones, strengths, abilities, and talents—allows you to discover the treasure of your Innate Inner Wisdom. Before you became centered and self-appreciative, your Innate Inner Wisdom was out of the range of your hearing. It was present with messages for you but your hearing was blocked with

self-limiting thoughts. You may have heard a little something and not known it's meaning, or how to decode or
interpret it. Now you can hear more fully. It is important
to know that your Innate Inner Wisdom has messages for
you 24/7, so you may need to slow down your perceiv-
ing in order to hear them. The channel is always open for
you to consult. Make full use of it and enjoy it.

## Following the inclination and direction of your Innate Inner Wisdom.

Your Inner Wise Self will enable you to make the best
choices for you in your life. Knowing that your Inner Wise
Voice is there for you to follow means any obstinance,
resistance, or rebelliousness can come to the surface so
that you can choose otherwise. Each step you take illu-
minates the next wise step, so on and on you go, making
one wise choice after another, and growing your trust
in your Inner Wise Voice. You no longer need to spend
time and energy debating choices. You can relax into this
self-trust. It's a new way of life.

## Self-Care as a way of life.

Following your Innate Inner Wisdom also reveals new ways of Self-Caring. It directs you to care for yourself in healthy ways without codependent behaviors. Your old ways, including saying *yes* when you wanted to say *no*, are replaced by saying *yes* to yourself as well as *no, thank you* to the other person. Self-Caring also replaces the need to do for others when they are best served by doing things for themselves.

Once you have become proficient in this type of Self-Caring, you experience an overflow of caring energy. This is a new resource available to share with others. You lose none of this energy when you share it. In fact, it is infinitely replenishable. You are freed to yet another level.

## Develop new, healthful routines.

Through the course of your reading this book, you developed the routine of relaxing your body to clear your mind. You also developed the routine of allowing yourself to open to new ideas. You have practiced breathing intentionally by taking in full breaths and letting go with each exhale. You have brought feelings into the room with the air and breathed them fully into your being.

Allow these new ways of being into every nuance of your life. Set the intention to do this, and the path will light up before you. Allow yourself to do these things again and again and over and over. It will be soothing. You have already established the foundation as you read this book. Now allow yourself to be drawn to revisit the chapters. Reading them again will open yet more doors for you.

Together, we have walked you up to and through the doorway of your Inner Freedom, which is the basis for Being Happy No Matter What.

What a path you are on! I hope you love every minute of it. The path is like no one else's. It's yours, and yours alone. Uniquely yours.

Allow yourself to be open to the ever-evolving insights now possible through your new eyes.

Soothing steps

Opening to allow

Easy pace

Relaxing first

Inner upset can actually be
used as a guide to Inner Freedom

Seeing things in a new way

PART V

# Resources

# New Thoughts to Remember

You are the star in your life

Retain credit for your feelings—the ones you
like and the ones you don't like—rather
than give away your power

The reaction I have to someone else's comments
comes from within myself

Everything is in the eye of the beholder

Appreciating myself and my ideas as a work of art

Appreciating me—all aspects of me

Masterpieces defy comparison

I am a unique, artistic masterpiece

Each moment of my life is a precious gift

I automatically set an aspect of my focus on the beauty that is in each moment of my life

The way I experience myself, situations, thoughts, and feelings is seen through the eyes of my lifetime understandings, and is colored by my original conclusions and decisions I made when I was a child

A liking vs. disliking approach is actually one of the most limiting approaches

All the decisions I have made were based on a bottom-line benefit for my life, even the decisions I haven't liked

I am the only one who chooses my attitude toward my experiences

All the decisions I have made, I made based on a benefit for my growth, even the decisions I have disliked

Healing occurs each time I relax

The more I relax my body, the clearer and more alert is my mind

There is a treasure within me: hearing my Inner Wisdom and acknowledging it

Appreciating my Inner Wisdom is also a treasure

There is transformative power in emphatically declaring an intention

My Inner Wisdom is communicating with me, whether I recognize it or not

To know me is to love me

I can cut other people slack on their feelings and not cut them slack on their disrespectful behavior

Accepting other people's feelings of disappointment or loss, and not accepting their disrespect or poor behavior, can both exist simultaneously

Opening to receive is a conscious decision

When I close off my Inner Wise Self, I close off
my thinking

When I habitually, inadvertently, ignorantly, and
even nobly and conscientiously close myself
off to receiving, I close off my access to my
Innate Inner Wisdom

The benefit of hindsight is to file the learning
for use in the future

When fear stops me from hearing my Inner Wise
Voice, I miss opportunities to get my needs met

I can learn to modulate my feelings

The capacity to change my experience is
within me

Following my Inner Wise Voice can lead me to
pleasant surprises

# Bedside Table Card for The Morning Call

Copy this statement onto an index card or even consider framing it to keep at your bedside.

THE MORNING CALL

## I Call My Inner Wisdom

I set the intention to access the treasure of my Inner Wisdom today.

# Learn More from Ellen

For information on talks, teaching intensives,

and retreats given by Ellen Seigel

and

To order calming and relaxing audio companions to

## Be Happy No Matter What
### 5 Steps to Inner Freedom

Visit www.BeHappyNoMatterWhat.com.

To book Ellen for a teaching event,

contact info@BeHappyNoMatterWhat.com

or call 614-842-4374.

## Special Bonus Gift

As a special thank-you to the readers of this book,

I would like to give you a free, downloadable,

audio-guided meditation.

To access this download, please visit

**www.BeHappyNoMatterWhat.com/bookbonus**

*From my heart to yours,*

*Ellen*

# About the Author

For over thirty years, Ellen has been working with
people to help them move efficiently and effectively
toward their goal of being happy no matter what
during and despite trying times in their lives. She
has created and presented programs, lectures,
and classes at the university level as well as for
professional associations of public school educators,
administrators, and health care practitioners at
national, state, and local levels. As an inspirational
public speaker, consultant, teacher, mentor, and life

and business coach, Ellen provides uniquely tailored approaches to accessing and utilizing hidden strengths and talents in those who want assistance.

Ellen earned her master's degree in social work from Yeshiva University in New York, acquired advanced training in hypnotherapy from the Wellness Institute in Seattle, and received an advanced certification in spirituality from Smith College. Ellen continues to enjoy the path of her own personal growth while living in Columbus, Ohio, with her husband. She can be reached through her website, www.BeHappyNoMatterWhat.com.

Notes

Notes

*Notes*

Notes

CPSIA information can be obtained at www.ICGtesting.com
Printed in the USA
LVOW05s0150170713

343170LV00005B/9/P